THUS SHALT THOU SERVE

D1150196

THUS SHALT THOU SERVE

*An Exposition
of the Offerings
and the Feasts
of Israel*

In Two Parts

by
CHARLES W. SLEMMING
D.D.

CHRISTIAN LITERATURE CRUSADE
Fort Washington, Pennsylvania 19034

CHRISTIAN LITERATURE CRUSADE

U.S.A.
P.O. Box 1449, Fort Washington, PA 19034

GREAT BRITAIN
51 The Dean, Alresford, Hants., SO24 9BJ

AUSTRALIA
P.O. Box 91, Pennant Hills, N.S.W. 2120

NEW ZEALAND
10 MacArthur Street, Feilding

This printing 1997

ISBN 0-87508-508-3

PRINTED IN THE UNITED STATES OF AMERICA

PREFACE

MUCH has been said concerning the tabernacle in the wilderness. It is a subject that has held a fascination for many Bible students, and yet in itself it is not complete.

One does not go to church these days to admire the architecture of the building, beautiful as some of them may be; nor yet to enjoy the comfort of the pews, for most pews are uncomfortable enough; neither does one go to church merely for the fellowship of friends, although this is rewarding. We go to church in order to worship God, to sing His praises, and to benefit from His Word.

Thus it was with the tabernacle. Interesting as it might have been as a structure, it was the service of the tabernacle that mattered. Having written on the tabernacle and on the priestly garments, we now add a third book to the series which, we trust, will bring enlightenment on the offerings and the feasts, or some of the ritual of the early Jewish worshipers. From these subjects we desire to see what God requires of us in our worship in these New Testament days.

We have already written two booklets on these subjects, but they are being withdrawn for a more comprehensive work put into a single volume. However, the book will be divided into Part I and Part II so that the subjects may be studied separately if desired. We trust that they may prove instructive and a blessing to the reader. Therefore we send this new book on its way, remembering that "*all* Scripture is given by inspiration of God, and is profitable."

Yours in the love of His Word,

C. W. SLEMMING.

London 1965.

CONTENTS

PART I
A Living Sacrifice
or *The Five Levitical Offerings*

PART II
Your Reasonable Service
or *The Feasts of the Lord*

A LIVING SACRIFICE

OR

THE FIVE LEVITICAL OFFERINGS

1

INTRODUCTION

A GREAT portion of the Book of Leviticus is given to the subject now coming under consideration. While the offerings all belonged to the immediate lives of the people and were observances, they were also commemorative, and had future fulfillment in the history of Israel; and then, beyond that, they foreshadowed some of the greatest doctrines of the church.

The offerings, with one exception, were sacrificial and required the shedding of blood. This was because they were figurative of the one sacrifice which was to be made once in the end of the age in the death of the Lord Jesus Christ. The feasts were not sacrificial but ceremonial. They revealed the present and future conduct of the people because they were, or would be, the people of God. We might define the two, therefore, by stating that the offerings were Godward and the feasts manward; or, as we have stated in another book, the offerings reveal man's walk *to* God through sacrifice, and the feasts declare man's walk *with* God through separation.

In all of these offerings, with their minute detail, it is discovered that nothing was left to man's imagination or interpretation, but to his obedience. The illustrations are perfect, requiring no additions or subtractions.

The holiness of God demanded a sacrifice.

The majesty of God required certain regulations.

The honor of God necessitated a code of conduct.

The perfection of God expected the best of its kind.

The purity of God deserved freedom from blemish.

The sovereignty of God meant absolute obedience to detail.

Five offerings were necessary because no one offering could give a complete picture of the perfect offering made in the end of the age, or cause us to understand all the significance, meaning, and blessings that were to come to the children of men from the one great and complete offering by our Lord Jesus Christ upon the cross of Calvary. Each was inadequate in itself, so five offerings revealed five different aspects of the one offering.

Chapter 1 is the Burnt Offering.

Chapter 2 is the Meal Offering.

Chapter 3 is the Peace Offering.

Chapter 4 is the Sin Offering.

Chapter 5 is the Trespass Offering.

In addition to the details given in the first five chapters are chapters 6 and 7 with the law of the offerings. Nothing was left to man's fancy or to human imagination. Every detail was dictated by God to Moses.

While the offerings are given in the order stated, it is to be noted that this was not the order in which they were observed—that was

(1) Burnt Offering.

(2) Meal Offering.

(3) Sin Offering.

(4) Trespass Offering.

(5) Peace Offering.

This change of order holds no significance with many people. Some may not have noticed that there was a difference, and others consider it as making "Much ado about nothing," suggesting that Moses on different occasions wrote them down as they came into his mind, as one might

jot down a shopping list from week to week. To this
attitude it must be pointed out that "*All* Scripture is given
by inspiration of God," not according to man's memory
or the failure of that memory. When things have an exact
repetition in the Bible we should take note of it, and when
variations reveal themselves these are just as noteworthy.
This is particularly important in these early chapters of
Leviticus because there appears to be such a lot of repetition about which Matthew 6:7 says: "But when ye pray,
use not vain repetitions, as the heathen do: for they think
that they shall be heard for their much speaking." As the
Bible does not contradict itself, whenever repetition is
found one may be sure that it is not "vain." Therefore
the reason must be found.

In this change of order, the peace offering, which was
third in the list, became fifth in the observance. It must be
the last of the five because peace comes as a result of
obeying all the others. Peace is effect, not cause. The
reason that it is third in the catalog is because the five
offerings are divided into two categories. The first three
are called sweet savor offerings, which means that they
were voluntary. As the peace offering was voluntary, it is
moved up with the other two in that class. Noah's offering
was a sweet savor offering (Gen. 8: 21). The last two
offerings were compulsory. God demanded a sin offering
and a trespass offering.

As surely as there was an order in which the offerings
were observed, so there was an order for the feasts, for
God is a God of order. This is well established in nature as
well as in His Word. Paul commanded the church to do all
things "decently and in order" (1 Cor. 14: 40).

Leviticus has ever been considered a dry and uninterest-
ing book, and not without reason. Many of the everyday
things of life and of nature are the same until we see them
under the microscope. Have you ever seen common salt,

sugar, or any other ordinary crystals, under a microscope? If not, you still have a great experience awaiting you. Have you seen grass, and the many minute forms of plant life which grow around us, under the microscope? If you have, you will know that these are some of those things of beauty which are a joy forever! It is our intention to put these truths of God's Word under the microscope of His Holy Spirit and to behold a detail and a wonder which some have never dreamed would be in the Bible, much less to be found in the Old Testament.

To simplify the studies, each offering will be divided similarly, considering

(1) *The Nature of the Offering*—that is, the animals used and why they were chosen.

(2) *The Offerer's Work.*

(3) *The Priest's Work.*

Then there is a division of the offerings, which includes

(4) *God's Portion.*

(5) *The Priest's Portion.*

(6) *The Offerer's Portion.*

After this will be a consideration of

(7) *The Typical Teaching,* as each offering points to that one Offering, the Lord Jesus Christ.

(8) *The Symbolism,* as it applies to the life of the believer.

All Scripture having been given by inspiration of God, the little details are as important as the great principles. Scanning the Bible may show its beauty and bring some satisfaction, but scrutinizing the Bible shows its wonder and creates a tremendous fascination. This is why we are encouraged to "search the scriptures," to "compare scripture with scripture," to "study to show ourselves approved unto God."

2

THE BURNT OFFERING

And the Lord called unto Moses, and spake unto him out of the tabernacle of the congregation, saying, Speak unto the children of Israel, and say unto them, If any man of you bring an offering unto the Lord, ye shall bring your offering of the cattle, even of the herd, and of the flock. If his offering be a burnt sacrifice of the herd, let him offer a male without blemish: he shall offer it of his own voluntary will at the door of the tabernacle of the congregation before the Lord. And he shall put his hand upon the head of the burnt offering; and it shall be accepted for him to make atonement for him. And he shall kill the bullock before the Lord: and the priests, Aaron's sons, shall bring the blood, and sprinkle the blood round about upon the altar that is by the door of the tabernacle of the congregation. And he shall flay the burnt offering, and cut it into his pieces. And the sons of Aaron the priest shall put fire upon the altar, and lay the wood in order upon the fire: and the priests, Aaron's sons shall lay the parts, the head, and the fat, in order upon the wood that is on the fire which is upon the altar: but his inwards and his legs shall he wash in water: and the priest shall burn all on the altar, to be a burnt sacrifice, an offering made by fire, of a sweet savour unto the Lord. And if his offering be of the flocks, namely, of the sheep, or of the goats, for a burnt sacrifice; he shall bring it a male without blemish. And he shall kill it on the side of the altar northward before the Lord: and the priests, Aaron's sons, shall sprinkle his blood round about upon the altar. And he shall cut it into his pieces, with his head and his fat: and the priest shall lay them in order on the wood that is on the fire which is upon the altar: but he shall wash the inwards and the legs with water: and the priest shall bring it all, and burn it upon the altar: it is a burnt sacrifice, an offering made by fire, of a sweet savour unto the Lord. And if the burnt sacrifice for his offering to the Lord be of fowls, then he shall bring his offering of turtledoves, or of young pigeons. And the priest shall bring it unto the altar, and wring off his head and burn it on the altar; and the blood thereof shall be wrung out at the side of the altar: and he shall pluck away his crop with his feathers, and cast it beside the altar on the east part, by the place of the ashes: and he shall cleave it with the wings thereof, but shall not divide it asunder: and the priest shall burn it upon the altar, upon the wood that is upon the fire: it is burnt sacrifice, an offering made by fire, of a sweet savour unto the Lord (Lev. 1:1–17).

And the Lord spake unto Moses, saying, Command Aaron and his sons, saying, This is the law of the burnt offering: It is the burnt offering, because of the burning upon the altar all night unto the morning, and the fire of the altar shall be burning in it. And the priest shall put on his linen garment, and his linen breeches shall be put upon his flesh, and take up the ashes which the fire hath consumed with the burnt offering on the altar, and he shall put them beside the altar. And he shall put off his garments, and put on other garments, and carry forth the ashes without the camp unto a clean place. And the fire upon the altar shall be burning in it; it shall not be put out: and the priest shall burn wood on it every morning, and lay the burnt offering in order upon it; and he shall burn thereon the fat of the peace offerings. The fire shall ever be burning upon the altar; it shall never go out (Lev. 6:8–13).

THIS first offering is called the burnt offering ". . . because of the burning upon the altar all night unto the morning, and the fire of the altar shall be burning in it. . . . And the fire upon the altar shall be burning in it; it shall not be put out: and the priest shall burn wood on it every morning, and lay the burnt offering in order upon it; and he shall burn thereon the fat of the peace offerings. The fire shall ever be burning upon the altar; and it shall never go out" (Lev. 6:9–13).

It is also called a sweet savor offering (Lev. 1:9 and 13). It has been pointed out in chapter 1 that the sweet savor offering signified a freewill offering. That statement is confirmed in Leviticus 1:3, ". . . he shall offer it of his own voluntary will."

While the offerings display the work that Christ accomplished upon the cross for the sinner as He dealt with his sin, his trespasses, and established his peace, yet we find in the burnt offering that Christ first meets God's holiness and satisfies His demands. He is "offering Himself without spot to God," doing the will of the Father, satisfying all His claims without any reservation on the Lord's part. In satisfying God's demands, secondly He meets man's need. This is why it is called a "whole burnt offering." It was given to God in its entirety, man having no share in it. At the same time it teaches that we in turn must surrender our best, yes, our all, seeking only to please Him who has called us. It is only to the extent in which we yield our all to Him that we shall learn to appreciate the fact that we are receiving His all in our lives. To the measure in which we seek to please Him we shall know those pleasures which are forevermore.

The Nature of the Offering—*According to possession. Bullocks, sheep, goats, turtledoves, pigeons.* "If his offering be a burnt sacrifice of the *herd*, let him offer a male without blemish..." (Lev. 1:3). "And if his offering be of the *flocks*, namely, of the sheep, or of the goats, for a burnt sacrifice; he shall bring it a male without blemish" (Lev. 1: 10). "And if the burnt sacrifice for his offering to the Lord be of *fowls,* then he shall bring his offering of turtledoves, or of young pigeons" (Lev. 1:14).

In each instance the animal was domestic, a creature that was tame and fed on vegetation, as against the wild animal and those which fed on carrion. Only the docile creature could represent the pure and holy One who gave His life a ransom for many. The animals had to be free from blemish as they prefigured the One who was free from sin.

Many today would denounce the idea of slaying an innocent animal, even though we slay innocent humans through our careless and selfish behavior on the highways, and appear to have no remorse for our appalling conduct. Man will murder his fellow-man in retaliation for the smallest injustice done to himself, or maybe because he desires excitement, and the law will do all it can to excuse the murderer. The religious views of the people of the world and their behavior are exceedingly conflicting, and even while some say that the shedding of blood should be removed, they are finding fault with Cain because he did not do that very thing; but the story of Cain and Abel reminds us that the slaying of an innocent animal existed long before the laws of Leviticus. As sin had already robbed man of life, nothing short of life could be the remedy.

Which of these animals should be offered by any particular offerer was not a matter of choice. The offering was

According to possession. If the social standing of the offerer were such that he was the possessor of *herd,* then he offered a bullock. God would not accept a lamb from him. If, however, the offerer did not possess herd but he did have *flock,* then his offering must be a sheep or a goat. Should the offerer be of the poor of the land, having neither herd nor flock, then the offering should be of *fowls*—turtledoves or young pigeons. This latter was the offering made by Mary, the Mother of Jesus, at the time of her purification, which is one of the indications that Jesus was born of poor parents.

The lesson indicated is that God expects man to give to Him to the measure that He has prospered him. He does not accept inferior gifts from those who have possessions, and neither does He expect from His people gifts, service, or anything that they do not possess. Our responsibilities are measured according to our privileges, not more than we have, not less than we have, always the best of what we have—without blemish.

In one instance there was an alternative, turtledoves or young pigeons. There might be little or no difference as to the monetary value of these birds. The alternative was due to the fact that at certain times of the year one or other of these birds would be out of season. It would then be tough and inedible. When they were of no use to man, they were of no use to the Lord. The birds had to be given when they were in season. Unless a thing costs us something it is worth nothing.

This is a very important lesson to learn. Man today is seeking to give God the things he does not want. The worn suit or the out-of-fashion dress are sent to the missionary. The unwanted furniture and the threadbare carpet are sent to the church for a rummage sale; or a man waits until he has made his fortune and has all that his heart desires, then he will offer his remaining years to the Lord's service. One is not suggesting that God cannot, or will not, use those years, but to the young man we would say: "Give your life while it is in season, with its energies and powers, and while the mind is clear and alert"; and to the older people God would say, since the missionary has given her all, could we not give her a new dress or something that is worthwhile? God asks for firstfruits, not leavings—for that which costs, not for that which is paltry—for that which honors His Name, not that which is an insult. "Ye offer polluted bread upon mine altar; and ye say, Wherein have we polluted thee? In that ye say, The table of the Lord is contemptible. And if ye offer the blind for sacrifice, is it not evil? and if ye offer the lame and sick, is it not evil? offer it now unto thy governor; will he be pleased with thee, or accept thy person? saith the Lord of hosts" (Mal. 1:7,8). "And ye brought that which was torn, and the lame, and the sick; thus ye brought an offering: should I accept this of your hand? saith the Lord" (Mal. 1:13). "And the King shall answer and say unto them, Verily I say unto you, Inasmuch as ye have done it unto one of the least of these my brethren, ye have done it unto me" (Matt. 25:40).

The Offerer's Work—*Identification.* ". . . he shall offer it of his own voluntary will at the door of the tabernacle of the congregation before the Lord" (Lev. 1:3).

This statement not only means that it was offered as a freewill gift, with no compulsion or pressure being put on the offerer (and compulsion always robs one of the joy of giving or the joy of service), but, according to the margin, it also reads "that he may be accepted." Comment has just been made on the quality of the gift. It is that which registers the quality of the giver. While the gift is important, the giver is more important to God—"that *he* may be accepted."

"And he shall put his hand upon the head of the burnt offering; and it shall be accepted for him to make atonement for him" (Lev. 1:4). The significance of this action is that he laid his hands heavily upon the living animal, as one would press heavily upon the seal of a document to leave the thumb imprint. It is identification. The animal was about to die, but before it did, the offerer identified himself with the living creature because he was going to be identified with the dead animal. In other words, he was recognizing that he was the one who should die and that this animal was his substitute.

Then he slew the animal. The offerer, or the sinner, is always the person responsible for death, for had there been no sin there would have been no death. "Wherefore, as by one man sin entered into the world, and death by sin; and so death passed upon all men, for that all have sinned" (Rom. 5:12).

With the bullocks and the birds there is no indication as to the exact spot of the sacrifice, but with the sheep it is stated that death was imposed on the north side of the altar. There is no reason why we should not believe that they were all slain in the same place. It is not necessary to make a repetition of words. However, the lamb is more specifically the type of Christ who was the Lamb of God, the One who took away the sins of the world, and He died on the north side of the city of Jerusalem. Calvary is located on the north of Jerusalem. It is amazing to see this detail in the law that was given 1,300 years before Christ died; and more amazing that the religious leaders of Christ's day, who were so steeped in the law, did not recognize the fulfilling of these scriptures. When the god of this world blinds men's eyes, they are surely blinded! Only the Lord can remove those scales.

The Priest's Work—*Sprinkling blood*. ". . . and the priests, Aaron's sons, shall bring the blood, and sprinkle the blood round about upon the altar that is by the door of the tabernacle of the congregation. And he shall flay the burnt offering, and cut it into his pieces. And the sons of Aaron the priest shall put fire upon the altar, and lay the wood in order upon the fire: and the priests, Aaron's sons, shall lay the parts, the head, and the fat, in order upon the wood that is on the fire which is upon the altar: but his inwards

and his legs shall he wash in water: and the priest shall burn
all on the altar, to be a burnt sacrifice . . ." (Lev. 1:5–9).

Seeing that Christ is the Burnt Offering, yielding His all
to the satisfaction of the Father, Aaron's sons would here
point to the Church of Jesus Christ because, as priests unto
God and as sons of the great High Priest, that Church is
the priestly household.

The priest had quite a duty to perform in this offering.
He had to

(1) "Sprinkle the blood round about upon the altar"
(Lev. 1: 5).

(2) "Flay the burnt offering" (Lev. 1: 6)

(3) "Cut it into his pieces" (Lev. 1: 6).

(4) "Put fire upon the altar, and lay the wood in order
upon the fire" (Lev. 1: 7).

(5) Wash the inwards and the legs (Lev. 1: 9).

(6) Burn the whole upon the altar (Lev. 1: 9).

(7) Wring off the head of the bird (Lev. 1: 15).

(8) Pluck away the crop and the feathers (Lev. 1: 16).

(9) Put on his linen garments (Lev. 6: 10).

(10) Carry forth the ashes without the camp (Lev. 6: 10,
11).

The believers, having accepted that the blood of Jesus
Christ (and the life is in the blood) has satisfied a Holy God
on their behalf, do not store that blood as some private
possession, but they, as priests, must distribute it around
in a way that others may see and recognize the same truth
and the same blood that has brought them cleansing. We
do not, and must not, scatter it just anywhere as something thrown away, because the blood is holy, it is precious, it must be kept within the sanctity of divine things.

Men were not permitted to eat blood because the life is
in it. Maybe the thought in mind would be clarified if we
considered the Name of Jesus. This, too, is precious on the
lips of believers, but when that same Name is scattered

around in the world outside it becomes a name used in blasphemy.

The flaying of the sacrifice was the skinning of the animal, thereby exposing the whole of the inwards and revealing that, within as well as without, it was free from blemish. Then the priest had to cut it into its pieces. This was not a chopping or a hacking of the carcase in some crude fashion, but a careful dissecting of the animal—the head, the inwards, the legs, to make sure that each part was free from any blemish. These parts were representative:

The head—the seat of the mind and the intellect.

The inwards—the will and the affections.

The legs—the outward walk and conduct.

The fat—health and virility.

When Christ our offering was thus examined, the results were:

In Him no sin (1 John 3: 5).

He knew no sin (2 Cor. 5: 21).

He did no sin (1 Pet. 2: 22).

He was without sin (Heb. 4: 15).

God said concerning His Son: "This is my beloved Son in whom I am well pleased." He satisfied His Father in thought, in word, in deed, in walk. We, too, as the Church, are encouraged to examine the nature and person of Christ as revealed in the Word. If we examine the head, we shall see that He came not to do His own will but the will of the Father. If we consider the fat, it would tell of His devotions and His affections finding them devoid of selfish interest. If we consider the inwards—the heart, the lungs, the kidneys, the liver—each doing a perfect job to maintain a perfect body, they would represent in Christ a heart of love, bowels of mercy, lungs of purity, the legs or limbs of a perfect walk.

Having been established as free from blemish, the sacrifice was then placed carefully and in order upon the fire and burned. Since there was no reservation, no imperfection, no selfish motive, and no self-glorification in Christ, God allowed Him to die, thereby satisfying His holiness.

The sacrifice of the burnt offering having been completed, the priest then had to attire in special garments and carry the ashes outside the camp into a clean place. Ashes are the result, or the fruit, of burning. These were carried with care to a special place because they had a special purpose. Salvation is the fruit of Christ's work on the cross. It must be acknowledged, propounded, kept separate from all else, by the Church because it and it alone can bring cleansing for the sinner.

God's Portion—*All that was burned.* That was the whole dissected carcase because it was a whole burnt offering; there was no reservation. It was the full consecration of the Lord Jesus Christ to God, the complete yieldedness of the Son to the Father. The other offerings were shared in one way or another; and yet, while this must remain true, there was

The Priest's Portion—*The skin.* Doctrinally all belonged to God. In type the priest had a portion inasmuch as he had a participation in the ceremony. The Word of God teaches "Do ye not know that they which minister about holy things live of the things of the temple? and they which wait at the altar are partakers with the altar? Even so hath the Lord ordained that they which preach the gospel should live of the gospel" (1 Cor. 9:13,14); also, ". . . the labourer is worthy of his hire . . ." (Luke 10:7).

The priest, therefore, received the skin, which is not referred to after the animal was flayed. It did not become part of the offering that was put on the fire and, therefore, not part of the "all that was burned." The skin was the evidence that the animal had existed. It was also the evidence of a sacrifice because there cannot be a skin without a sacrifice. Would not this skin, the only property of man, take our minds back to the Garden of Eden and to the skin which God provided for a covering for Adam and Eve?

The Offerer's Portion—*Nothing.* The offerer shared only in one offering, the peace offering. As a sinner man has no participation in the work of redemption because salvation is not the result of our works but of His work.

The Typical Teaching—*Christ our Passover. Surrender of self.* As no one offering could give a full-length portrait of the great offering, the Lord Jesus Christ, five offerings were needful to reveal five aspects of His perfect work. The burnt offering, as the first of these five offerings, reveals the work of the Son toward the Father before the work of the Saviour toward mankind. It is the complete consecration of the whole being of the Son of God to the will, mind, and purposes of God, which brought complete satisfaction to the heart of God. Said He: "I came down from heaven, not to do mine own will, but the will of him that sent me" (John 6:38). "My meat is to do the will of him that sent me, and to finish his work" (John 4:34). "... Christ also hath loved us, and hath given himself for us an offering and a sacrifice to God for a sweetsmelling savour" (Eph. 5:2). "How much more shall the blood of Christ, who through the eternal Spirit offered himself without spot to God, purge your conscience from dead works to serve the living God?" (Heb. 9:14).

The Symbolism—*Consecration of self.* This is the truth as it applies itself to mankind, or what God intends us to understand from the pictures He draws and the demonstrations He performs.

In the burnt offering it was the complete and entire consecration of the offerer to God. As Jesus offered Himself to God without any reservation, so in turn must we do the same thing. Thus the apostle declared: "I beseech you therefore, brethren, by the mercies of God, that ye present your bodies a living sacrifice, holy, acceptable unto

God, which is your reasonable service" (Rom. 12:1). "For ye are bought with a price: therefore glorify God in your body, and in your spirit, which are God's" (1 Cor. 6:20).

Man takes one step at a time not only in his comprehension of spiritual things but also in his Christian walk. It must always be appreciated that steps must be taken in the right order. The first step is always before the second step, and so on. To stand on the top rung of the ladder, it had to be reached by mounting one by one the lower rungs. To stand in the place of spiritual reception and enjoy all that He is giving, we must first surrender our whole being in a complete yieldedness to the Lord, as Jesus yielded Himself without reserve to His Father.

3

THE MEAL OFFERING

And when any will offer a meat offering unto the Lord, his offering shall be of fine flour; and he shall pour oil upon it, and put frankincense thereon: and he shall bring it to Aaron's sons the priests: and he shall take thereout his handful of the flour thereof, and of the oil thereof, with all the frankincense thereof; and the priest shall burn the memorial of it upon the altar, to be an offering made by fire, of a sweet savour unto the Lord: and the remnant of the meat offering shall be Aaron's and his sons': it is a thing most holy of the offerings of the Lord made by fire. And if thou bring an oblation of a meat offering baken in the oven, it shall be unleavened cakes of fine flour mingled with oil, or unleavened wafers anointed with oil. And if thy oblation be a meat offering baken in a pan, it shall be of fine flour un-leavened, mingled with oil. Thou shalt part it in pieces, and pour oil thereon: it is a meat offering. And if thy oblation be a meat offering baken in the fryingpan, it shall be made of fine flour with oil. And thou shalt bring the meat offering that is made of these things unto the Lord: and when it is presented unto the priest, he shall bring it unto the altar. And the priest shall take from the meat offering a memorial thereof, and shall burn it upon the altar: it is an offering made by fire, of a sweet savour unto the Lord. And that which is left of the meat offer-ing shall be Aaron's and his sons': it is a thing most holy of the offerings of the Lord made by fire. No meat

26 THUS SHALT THOU SERVE

offering, which ye shall bring unto the Lord, shall be made with leaven: for ye shall burn no leaven, nor any honey, in any offering of the Lord made by fire. As for the oblation of the firstfruits, ye shall offer them unto the Lord: but they shall not be burnt on the altar for a sweet savour. And every oblation of thy meat offering shalt thou season with salt; neither shalt thou suffer the salt of the covenant of thy God to be lacking from thy meat offering: with all thine offerings thou shalt offer salt. And if thou offer a meat offering of thy firstfruits unto the Lord, thou shalt offer for the meat offering of thy firstfruits green ears of corn dried by the fire, even corn beaten out of full ears. And thou shalt put oil upon it, and lay frankincense thereon: it is a meat offering. And the priest shall burn the memorial of it, part of the beaten corn thereof, and part of the oil thereof, with all the frankincense thereof: it is an offering made by fire unto the Lord (Lev. 2:1–16).

And this is the law of the meat offering: the sons of Aaron shall offer it before the Lord, before the altar. And he shall take of it his handful, of the flour of the meat offering, and of the oil thereof, and all the frankincense which is upon the meat offering, and shall burn it upon the altar for a sweet savour, even the memorial of it, unto the Lord. And the remainder thereof shall Aaron and his sons eat: with unleavened bread shall it be eaten in the holy place; in the court of the tabernacle of the congregation they shall eat it. It shall not be baken with leaven. I have given it unto them for their portion of my offerings made by fire; it is most holy, as is the sin offering, and as the trespass offering. All the males among the children of Aaron shall eat of it. It shall be a statute for ever in your generations concerning the offerings of the Lord made by fire: every one that toucheth them shall be holy (Lev. 6:14–18).

ALTHOUGH this is called the meat offering in our Authorized Version, it was the only offering of the five which made no use of flesh whatsoever. Instead the ingredients were cereal. The reason for using the word "meat" was that, in the days when King James ruled England (the days when this version was prepared), a person would not be asked out to a "meal." He would be invited to "meat." So the word "meal" offering will be used throughout, which would be correct in present-day understanding.

Three different expressions are used in describing the offerings. They are "sacrifice," "oblation," and "offering." All of these have their place, and are not merely alternatives all meaning the same thing.

Sacrifice. This always involved the shedding of blood. Living animals full of life and free from blemish were slain. This signified a life surrendered.

Oblation. This had nothing to do with blood, and referred to the offering of grain, flour, cakes, and the first-fruits of harvest.

Offering is a general term expressive of both, inasmuch as both were offered by one person to another.

The Hebrew word for meal offering is *minchah,* meaning "the gift of an inferior to a superior." The word is sometimes translated "present," as in the "present" sent by Jacob to Esau, also the "present" to Joseph from his brethren. *Minchah* is likewise translated "offering" in the story of Cain and Abel.

Two of these references must be enlarged upon in order to establish the full meaning of this word *minchah* because it affects Biblical interpretation. Let us repeat that *minchah* means "the gift of an inferior to a superior," for it will be appreciated that such a gift must be worthy of the one to whom it is presented. If the gift were to be made to the Queen of England, or to the President of the United States of America, it must be worthy of the person or of the office held. Better give no gift than one which is inferior, because then it becomes an insult.

Jacob was commanded by God to return to his home-
land and his family. On his way he learned that Esau was
coming to meet him and that he was accompanied by 400
men. This was the Esau whom Jacob had twice wronged
and from whom he had earlier fled. He was now fearful of
the brother from whom he had stolen both blessing and
birthright. Jacob prayed to God and confessed his unworthiness but asked for the Lord's delivering grace. After
that he prepared a present for his brother (Gen. 32:13).
This present was the same *minchah* of our study. The
instructions given by Jacob to his servants, when they met
Esau and offered his gift, were: "They be thy *Servant*
Jacob's; it is a *present* sent unto my *lord* Esau" (Gen.
32:18). This was the first time that Jacob had humiliated
himself before Esau. It is true that fear was the motive, but
we are establishing the meaning of *minchah,* the offering
we are preparing to study.

There is yet another valuable lesson to learn. It is in the
story of Cain and Abel. It is generally conceded that God
accepted the offering of Abel because of the blood, and
rejected the offering of Cain because the fruit of the earth
was an evidence of works. However, all the facts of the
case do not support this interpretation.

(1) There is no Biblical evidence that Adam and Eve
ever offered a sacrifice.

(2) There is no Biblical evidence that God had required
one up to that moment.

(3) Cain and Abel were the children of Adam and Eve,
so we are still at the very beginning of the human race.

(4) The coats of skin were God's provision, not His
requirement at that juncture.

(5) If this offering were a *minchah,* and it was, then it
was the meal offering and no flesh or blood were part of it.

(6) If we assert "the fruit of the ground" was that which
represented works, then surely sheep are the results of the

labors of a shepherd as fruit is the result of the toil of the farmer!

What the Lord would have us learn from this account is not the quality of the offering, but the character of the offerer. ". . .Cain brought of the fruit of the ground. . ." (Gen. 4:3). "And Abel, he also brought of the firstlings of his flock and the fat thereof " (Gen. 4:4). The fat was the choicest part of the animal and was always required by God, as is repeated in Leviticus. Everything in the two verses suggests that Cain took the first to come to hand, and Abel with care chose the best of his flock. If one reads carefully the rest of the verse, it will be discovered that this is the fact of the case: "And the Lord *had respect unto Abel* and to his offering." God did not accept Abel because of his offering. God received the offering because of Abel. He was a man with a right heart and a right motive, and God does not look on the outward appearance. He looks on the heart.

With this as introduction, the meal offering will now be considered.

The Nature of the Offering—*According to property. Uncooked flour, unleavened cakes, roasted grain.* In each offering there were alternatives, not for the convenience of the offerer, as might be supposed, but according to the circumstances of the offerer, and, of course, according to the command of God.

Uncooked flour, or flour in the raw. As it was received so it could be given, remembering that this offering typified services. Man can give back to God. He has life, he may give it to God; he has time, he may give a portion; he has a Bible, he can read it; he can attend church, sing with the congregation, contribute to the collection, give a little service here and there which he feels capable of doing. God will accept these.

Unleavened cakes. Here some effort had been used to

turn the flour into something that was edible and tasty, and something which could be shared with others. The life here has become a yielded life, the time given is made as effective as can be. The Bible is not just read, it is studied, kneaded, mixed with experience which makes it appetizing food. Church attendance becomes church service. The voice is developed so that it can be used to His glory. It could find its way into the choir for others to share the enjoyment. It is no more dropping a coin into the plate but learning to tithe. It is not the odd job but the dedicated service. This is more acceptable to God. All this is to be done without the leaven of pride or self-esteem.

Roasted grain, that which is preserved by fire. The faith that has stood the fire of trial, the promises of God that have been tested and tried, the life that has come through severe temptations and proved God to be faithful, are things which rejoice the heart of God. "That the trial of your faith, being much more precious than of gold that perisheth, though it be tried with fire, might be found unto praise and honour and glory at the appearing of Jesus Christ" (1 Pet. 1:7).

As in the burnt offering, so in the meal offering there is a division of requirement concerning the offerer. In the first it was according to possession, in the second

According to property. What he offered was ascertained by the fact of possessing an *oven, a pan* (baking-pan), or a *fryingpan.*

Attached to these offerings were certain restrictions. "No meat offering, which ye shall bring unto the Lord, shall be made with leaven: for ye shall burn no leaven, nor any honey, in any offering of the Lord made by fire" (Lev. 2:11).

No leaven. Leaven is always a type of sin. It is that which, when brought into contact with fire, throws the lump into risings and commotions. The fermenting properties of leaven reduce the whole of the meal into a condition of corruption. ". . . Know ye not that a little leaven leaveneth the whole lump? Purge out therefore the old leaven, that ye may be a new lump, as ye are unleavened" (1 Cor. 5:6,7). "How is it that ye do not understand that I spake it not to you concerning bread, that ye should beware of the leaven of the Pharisees and of the Sadducees? Then understood they how that he bade them not beware of the leaven of bread, but of the doctrine of the Pharisees and of the Sadducees" (Matt. 16:11,12).

Do not overlook that in this meal offering service is being considered more than salvation. There was no selfish intent, no malice, no evil thought in the ministry of Christ, as there was no sin in Him. Likewise for the believer, there must be no malice in his life and no ill motive in his service. Everything must be done with singleness of purpose if it is to be accepted by God.

No *honey*. Honey, although sweet to the taste, if taken in excess can turn sour in the stomach. The pleasures of life are only for a season; they soon fail. "It is not good to eat much honey" (Prov. 25:27). Dr. V. Raymond Edman points out that roasted barley without sweetening is tasteless. The things that speak of Christ's suffering must not have man's ideas added to them in order to make them more palatable to us. It is necessary constantly to remind oneself of what it meant to Him, the Holy One, to bear away our sin. If we, as Christians, would spend more time contemplating what it cost Him for our redemption, we would spend less time counting how much it costs us to serve Him. Was there any sorrow like unto His sorrow?

Then there was the addition of some condiments.

Salt. "And every oblation of thy meat offering shalt thou season with salt; neither shalt thou suffer the salt of the covenant of thy God to be lacking from thy meat offering: with all thine offerings thou shalt offer salt. . .

And thou shalt put oil upon it, and lay frankincense there-on: it is a meat offering" (Lev. 2:13,15).

Salt holds many symbols. Two are referred to in verse 13, the salt of seasoning and the salt of the covenant. The salt of purification is not missing from the meaning of the verse. "And every oblation of thy meat offering shalt thou season with salt." This is the salt that brings out the true flavor of a thing so that it may be enjoyed to the full.

It has been observed that the leaven (corruption) had to be missing. Now the purity of the offering became more sure by the addition of salt, because salt is that which checks corruption and any form of putrefaction. It helps to maintain health.

"Neither shalt thou suffer the salt of the covenant of thy God to be lacking from thy meat offering. . . ."

There were three covenants observed by the bedouin of the desert. They were the covenant of bread and wine, the covenant of salt, and the covenant of blood. The people of God were in the desert at this time and would be familiar with these things. God here introduced the second of these covenants, which established a relationship of friendship between bedouins. Other references to this covenant of salt are to be found in the Old Testament. "All the heave offerings of the holy things, which the children of Israel offer unto the Lord, have I given thee, and thy sons and thy daughters with thee, by a statute for ever: it is a covenant of salt for ever before the Lord unto thee and to thy seed with thee" (Num. 18:19). "Ought ye not to know that the Lord God of Israel gave the kingdom over Israel to David for ever, even to him and to his sons by a covenant of salt?" (2 Chron. 13:5).

The statement in Lev. 2:13, therefore, means "I present this gift because of the covenanted relationship in which I stand before Jehovah." This same thought is conveyed in the New Testament where it states: "Let your speech be

alway with grace, seasoned with salt, that ye may know
how ye ought to answer every man" (Col. 4:6). As Christians, we should so behave and conduct ourselves that we
will be declaring to the world that we are a people who are
in a covenant relationship with the Lord.

Frankincense. This is a spice that becomes effective
through burning. It denoted prayer and intercession. A
life work of effective service must be steeped in prayer.
The most prayerful life spent on earth was that of the
Lord Jesus Christ, who often spent whole nights in prayer.
Fire caused the odor to rise, as trials, which drive us to
our knees, cause our prayers to ascend to God.

The Offerer's Work—*Bring to priest.* "And he shall bring
it to Aaron's sons the priests" (Lev. 2:2).

Having prepared the offering as instructed, he now
brought it to the priests and handed it over in its entirety.
This was done at the door of the tabernacle. There was no
ceremony, no participation, just a simple yieldedness for
there was nothing meritorious in his action, only obedience. In all the service we render to the Lord none of it is
to declare our worthiness, to display our merits, or to
purchase our salvation. Service is a privilege, not a remuneration.

The Priest's Work—*Offer a handful.* He received the
meal offering from the offerer, took from it a handful of
the meal, grain, or cakes, with all the frankincense, and
burned it on the altar. The remainder belonged to the
priests. It was eaten by Aaron and his sons in the court of
the tabernacle.

God's Portion—*The handful.* The handful of meal and
all the frankincense were His. Only a small portion of this
offering belonged to God but it was a memorial, which
means that the handful represented the whole in the sight
of God and was accepted by Him as the whole.

Has it ever occurred to us that a very small portion of

what we give to God, in both gifts and service, really belongs to Him? We give our tithes and our offerings, placing them in a collection plate or box. They become our gifts to God and yet they are taken and given to man—the minister's salary, the janitor's wages, the lighting and heating bills, the advertising, the repair and maintenance of the buildings. Other gifts go to missionary funds for fares, salaries, office staff, etc., until it would appear that God receives nothing from our giving; but He does, inasmuch as He recognizes it, for by its means His work must go on.

Not only money but service can be self-centered. We spend more time in church activities, in making pictures and illustrations for children, in having clubs and outings for young people, in social events in the church, in hymn singing, choirs, solos, trumpets, and comparatively a small portion of the time in actually teaching God's Word.

However, there is a handful which does belong exclusively to God, a portion in which man can have no part—that is, worship. May we, therefore, never become so active in service that we have no time for worship. "But the hour cometh, and now is, when the true worshippers shall worship the Father in spirit and in truth: for the Father seeketh such to worship him" (John 4:23).

The Priest's Portion—*The remainder.* All that remained after the handful had been removed. His time was occupied with the things of God. He had separated himself from the world to that end. The world contributes nothing to the support of the ministry; therefore the Church must. The Christian has a responsibility before God of providing that which is necessary for the support of God's servants. God not only declared it but in his law He made provision for it. It is part of our service. Some of God's people are very generous in this respect, but others are more mean in their relationship with God than they are with their friends. They will pay entrance fees for everything they want to see and enjoy, but give nothing to the church from which they are receiving all of their spiritual food and their fellowship.

The priest had to partake of his portion within the court of the tabernacle.

The Offerer's Portion—*Nothing.* God only accepts that which is wholehearted and is willingly given. Ananias and Sapphira failed and perished because of a partiality which wrought deception. All our service must be done with singleness of eye unto the Lord. All the glory must be His also. The blessing becomes ours.

The Typical Teaching—*The corn of wheat.* Each offering points to the Lord Jesus Christ and declares some attribute of that great offering made once in the end of the age. In the meal offering Christ is seen as the corn of wheat which fell into the ground and died that He might bring forth much fruit. He was also the corn of wheat which went through the crushing mill of Gethsemane and the fierce oven of Calvary to become the Bread of Life, the sustainer of His people on a pilgrim journey. He gave His all. He knew no reservation. He came not to be ministered unto but to minister and to give His life a ransom for many, and now upon Him we feed and find our source of strength.

The Symbolism—*Consecration of gifts. Consecration of service.* The great truth to be noted is the order that God has set forth. In the burnt offering it was the consecration of self. In the meal offering it was the consecration of service, and it is always in that order throughout Scripture. We cannot give our service until we have given ourselves, and when we have given ourselves we are then to give our service. Should these be placed in reverse order so that service comes first, we might find ourselves giving our service as a means of purchasing salvation, but this cannot be. Our works do not precede us for salvation, but our works do *follow* us. They have a place and they have reward. Hence we work out our salvation although we cannot work it in. The same truth is taught throughout the Word of God. In the New Testament the Lord said: "Therefore if thou bring thy gift to the altar, and there rememberest that thy brother hath ought against thee; leave there thy gift before the altar, and go thy way; first be reconciled to thy brother, and then come and offer thy gift" (Matt. 5:23,24)—reconciliation with the brother before presentation of gifts. God's requirement of man is reconciliation with Himself before the presentation of any gift or service.

Maybe the most beautiful illustration of this great truth has been lost in the fog of tradition. It belongs to the Christmas story and concerns the Wise Men who brought their gifts to the newborn King. The gifts brought on that occasion were four, and the most important one has been lost because we are ever speaking of and singing about the "three wise men from Orient far." They are seen everywhere on Christmas cards and in Christmas decorations, in church and commercial world alike; but from whence have these *three* wise men come? Certainly not from the scriptural narrative because that says: ". . . behold, there came wise men from the east to Jerusalem, saying, Where is he that is born King of the Jews? for we have seen his star in the east, and are come to worship him" (Matt. 2:1,2). The number has been concluded from the number of gifts, but such is inconclusive because more than one person could carry either gold, frankincense, or myrrh.

According to protocol, when children are born to reigning monarchs all other kings, queens, and rulers of the world recognize these births by sending gifts. This is still done to the present day. When Jesus was born King of the Jews, protocol required that gifts should be sent. This is what these Wise Men were expected to do, but they did not. Instead of *sending* their gifts, they took a long tedious journey across the desert on the backs of camels, "And when they were come into the house, they saw the young child with Mary His mother, and *fell down, and worshipped him:* and when they had opened their treasures, *they presented unto him gifts:* gold, and frankincense, and myrrh" (Matt. 2:11).

The very first gift they offered was themselves. Instead of sending gifts by servants, they came and *fell down and worshipped.* It was an act of adoration, an act of humiliation, and an act of surrender of themselves. After this most important surrender of self, they presented unto Him their material gifts.

4

THE SIN OFFERING

And the Lord spake unto Moses, saying, Speak unto the children of Israel saying, If a soul shall sin through ignorance against any of the commandments of the Lord concerning things which ought not to be done, and shall do against any of them: if the priest that is anointed do sin according to the sin of the people; then let him bring for his sin, which he hath sinned, a young bullock without blemish unto the Lord for a sin offering. And he shall bring the bullock unto the door of the tabernacle of the congregation before the Lord; and shall lay his hand upon the bullock's head, and kill the bullock before the Lord. And the priest that is anointed shall take of the bullock's blood, and bring it to the tabernacle of the congregation: and the priest shall dip his finger in the blood, and sprinkle of the blood seven times before the Lord, before the vail of the sanctuary. And the priest shall put some of the blood upon the horns of the altar of sweet incense before the Lord, which is in the tabernacle of the congregation; and shall pour all the blood of the bullock at the bottom of the altar of the burnt offering, which is at the door of the tabernacle of the congregation. And he shall take off from it all the fat of the bullock for the sin offering; the fat that covereth the inwards, and all the fat that is upon the inwards, and the two kidneys, and the fat that is upon them, which is by the flanks, and the caul above the liver, with the kidneys, it shall he take away, as it was taken off from the

bullock of the sacrifice of peace offerings: and the priest
shall burn them upon the altar of the burnt offering.
And the skin of the bullock, and all his flesh, with his
head, and with his legs, and his inwards, and his dung,
even the whole bullock shall he carry forth without the
camp unto a clean place, where the ashes are poured
out, and burn him on the wood with fire: where the
ashes are poured out shall he be burnt. And if the whole
congregation of Israel sin through ignorance, and the
thing be hid from the eyes of the assembly, and they
have done somewhat against any of the commandments
of the Lord concerning things which should not be
done, and are guilty; when the sin, which they have
sinned against it, is known, then the congregation shall
offer a young bullock for the sin, and bring him before
the tabernacle of the congregation. And the elders of
the congregation shall lay their hands upon the head of
the bullock before the Lord: and the bullock shall be
killed before the Lord. And the priest that is anointed
shall bring of the bullock's blood to the tabernacle of the
congregation: and the priest shall dip his finger in some
of the blood, and sprinkle it seven times before the
Lord, even before the vail. And he shall put some of the
blood upon the horns of the altar which is before the
Lord, that is in the tabernacle of the congregation, and
shall pour out all the blood at the bottom of the altar of
the burnt offering, which is at the door of the tabernacle
of the congregation. And he shall take all his fat from
him, and burn it upon the altar. And he shall do with the
bullock as he did with the bullock for a sin offering, so
shall he do with this: and the priest shall make an atonement for them, and it shall be forgiven them. And he
shall carry forth the bullock without the camp, and burn
him as he burned the first bullock: it is a sin offering for
the congregation. When a ruler hath sinned, and done
somewhat through ignorance against any of the commandments of the Lord his God concerning things
which shall not be done, and is guilty; or if his sin,

wherein he hath sinned, come to his knowledge; he shall bring his offering, a kid of the goats, a male without blemish: and he shall lay his hand upon the head of the goat, and kill it in the place where they kill the burnt offering before the Lord: it is a sin offering. And the priest shall take of the blood of the sin offering with his finger, and put it upon the horns of the altar of burnt offering, and shall pour out his blood at the bottom of the altar of burnt offering. And he shall burn all his fat upon the altar, as the fat of the sacrifice of peace offerings: and the priest shall make an atonement for him as concerning his sin, and it shall be forgiven him. And if any one of the common people sin through ignorance, while he doeth somewhat against any of the commandments of the Lord concerning things which ought not to be done, and be guilty; or if his sin, which he hath sinned, come to his knowledge: then he shall bring his offering, a kid of the goats, a female without blemish, for his sin which he hath sinned. And he shall lay his hand upon the head of the sin offering, and slay the sin offering in the place of the burnt offering. And the priest shall take of the blood thereof with his finger, and put it upon the horns of the altar of burnt offering, and shall pour out all the blood thereof at the bottom of the altar. And he shall take away all the fat thereof, as the fat is taken away from off the sacrifice of peace offerings; and the priest shall burn it upon the altar for a sweet savour unto the Lord; and the priest shall make an atonement for him, and it shall be forgiven him. And if he bring a lamb for a sin offering, he shall bring it a female without blemish. And he shall lay his hand upon the head of the sin offering, and slay it for a sin offering in the place where they kill the burnt offering. And the priest shall take of the blood of the sin offering with his finger, and put it upon the horns of the altar of burnt offering, and shall pour out all the blood thereof at the bottom of the altar: and he shall take away all the fat thereof, as the fat of the lamb is taken away from the sacrifice of the peace offerings; and the priest shall burn them upon the altar, according to the offerings made by fire unto the Lord: and the priest shall make an atonement for his sin that he hath committed, and it shall be forgiven him (Lev. 4:2–35).

And the Lord spake unto Moses, saying, Speak unto Aaron and to his sons, saying, This is the law of the sin offering: In the place where the burnt offering is killed shall the sin offering be killed before the Lord: it is most holy. The priest that offereth it for sin shall eat it: in the holy place shall it be eaten in the court of the tabernacle of the congregation. Whatsoever shall touch the flesh thereof shall be holy: and when there is sprinkled of the blood thereof upon any garment, thou shalt wash that whereon it was sprinkled in the holy place. But the earthen vessel wherein it is sodden shall be broken: and if it be sodden in a brasen pot, it shall be both scoured, and rinsed in water. All the males among the priests shall eat thereof: it is most holy. And no sin offering, whereof any of the blood is brought into the tabernacle of the congregation to reconcile withal in the holy place, shall be eaten: it shall be burnt in the fire (Lev. 6:24–30).

IT HAS already been pointed out that the peace offering was last in the list of observances but third in the classification of these Levitical chapters. In these studies it is being placed last. Therefore, the sin offering is now to be considered. This is the first of the two compulsory offerings.

The Nature of the Offering—*According to position. Bullock, goat, or lamb.* These differed from the animals of the burnt offering inasmuch as there were no fowls. The variation of the animals in this offering was

According to position. These are designated.

(1) *Priest.* "If the *priest* that is anointed do sin according to the sin of the people; then let him bring for his sin,

which he hath sinned, a young bullock without blemish unto the Lord for a sin offering" (Lev. 4:3).

(2) *Whole congregation.* "And if the whole congregation of Israel sin through ignorance .. when the sin, which they have sinned against it, is known, then the congregation shall offer a young bullock for the sin, and bring him before the tabernacle of the congregation" (Lev. 4:13,14).

(3) *Ruler.* "When a ruler hath sinned, and done somewhat through ignorance against any of the commandments of the Lord his God concerning things which should not be done, and is guilty; . . . he shall bring his offering, a kid of the goats, a male without blemish" (Lev. 4:22,23).

(4) *Commoner.* "And if any one of the common people sin through ignorance, . . . then he shall bring his offering, a kid of the goats, a female without blemish, for his sin which he hath sinned" (Lev. 4:27,28).

In these classifications it is to be seen that:

A priest offered a bullock.

The whole congregation offered a bullock.

The ruler offered a male goat.

The commoner offered a female goat.

The offerings required by God for the priest and the whole congregation were equal, or, in the sight of God the sin of a priest was as large as the sin of a whole congregation, because if a man in an official capacity sins, he can lead a whole nation astray. It was Trapp, one of the old divines, who said: "If a teacher sins he teaches sin." High position means high responsibility. If you are a pastor, a teacher, a Bible class leader, a deacon, if you hold any church office, then you have to be extra careful in your conduct because others are taking you as an example.

The offering of a ruler was a male, which is a symbol of authority, but with a commoner, who had no authority, the offering was a female. In each instance the sacrifice had to be perfect, without blemish, because it foreshadowed the perfect Sacrifice. The difference lay in the treatment of the blood and in the disposition of the carcass.

Four times "through ignorance" is repeated. Responsibility is not pushed aside so easily. In our civil laws the powers that be never seem to listen to our pleas of ignorance. If we have broken the law we pay the price. How much more with God? Ignorance is not easily established; much of the ignorance we seek to claim is willful. We could have found the facts but we did not bother.

The Offerer's Work—*Identify himself. To slay the sacrifice.* This offering had to be made at the gate of the tabernacle court, which was the place of God's choosing. God did not permit this sacrifice for sin to be made just anywhere. This would have led to uncontrolled practices, idolatry, the establishment of sacred sites. In fact, all these things are with us today. The Cross is being replaced by ceremonial practices. The church, as an organism, is being substituted by organization. The Bible is being pushed aside for creeds and credentials.

The offerer then placed his hands heavily upon the head of the animal. In the case of the whole nation having sinned, this would be done by the elders who would be their representatives. This act had a twofold significance. In the first place, it was one of identification. They identified themselves as one with the animal that was about to die, even as by the act of placing our thumb impression upon a document we identify ourselves with that document. Secondly, it was an act of imputation. They believed that their sins passed from them to the animal, so that, when it died, it would be in their place.

The offerer then slew the animal. He was the one who had sinned, and therefore he was the one who was responsible for the death of the animal. It is easy to blame

the Jewish nation for the death of Jesus. Anyone can lay
the charge against Pilate who condemned, or the Roman
soldiers who crucified, but it was our sins that nailed Him
to the tree.

The Priest's Work—*Sprinkling blood.* He took the blood
of the sin offering into the Holy Place and sprinkled it
seven times before the Lord, before the veil of the
sanctuary. This would signify God's acceptance. After this,
as he came out, he applied the blood here and there. The
order is beautifully set forth—before the Lord, before the
veil, upon the altar of incense, at the brazen altar of
sacrifice where the remainder was poured out.

The picture is that of the blood being applied as he came
out, not as he went in. Salvation is of the Lord. The way was
opened from God to man. It was opened by our great High
Priest, the Lord Jesus Christ. It was opened through the
shedding of His blood, and along that bloodstained way
man travels from without to within. We meet Christ at
Calvary, where He poured out His soul an offering for
sin; then we proceed to the golden altar, the place of His
intercession, and on to the veil now rent, giving us access
into the presence of the eternal God where we have a
perfect standing before Him.

In the event of the offering being that of a ruler or
commoner, the blood remained outside.

The priest then took all the fat of the inwards and
burned it upon the altar (the significance of the fat will be
found in Chapter 6 concerning the peace offering).

Having dealt with the blood, then came the disposal of
the carcass. This must have seemed extraordinary to the
priest who had to take the whole of it and carry it outside
the camp to the place where he poured the ashes. There
were very strict conditions under which it was carried out.
"And the skin of the bullock, and all his flesh, with his
head, and with his legs, and his inwards, and his dung, even

the whole bullock shall he carry forth without the camp unto a clean place, where the ashes are poured out, and burn him on the wood with fire: where the ashes are poured out shall he be burnt" (Lev. 4:11,12). "And no sin offering, whereof any of the blood is brought into the tabernacle of the congregation to reconcile withal in the holy place, shall be eaten: it shall be burnt in the fire" (Lev. 6:30).

All this was ordained by God because He intended them to understand the severity of His judgment on sin. Sin was now in this animal by reason of imputation, so it must be carried away carefully and destroyed totally. This was known as

God's Portion—*The whole.* No part of this animal was for man. No part of it could be used as food. We live in a day when we have lost the sense of the holiness of God, His sovereignty, and His severity. All the judgment of our sin fell upon the Son of His love when He, who knew no sin, became sin and died in our place. This price that was paid cost God the very best that He had—His Only Begotten Son, He who was in the bosom of the Father in a past eternity. No wonder there is no mercy for sin outside of Christ's redeeming work!

Yet, despite all these things, part of the sacrifice did become

The Priest's Portion—*Part of commoner's.* The priest was always rewarded for the service rendered. However, his part came from the offering of the ruler or commoner, never part of the priest's or the congregation's, because he could be a partaker of such sins. He had a share of the sheep or goat, but never of the bullock. This is gathered from the fact that the carcass of the sheep or goat was not carried outside. "The priest that offereth it for sin shall eat it: in the holy place shall it be eaten, in the court of the tabernacle of the congregation" (Lev. 6:26).

Even so, the vessels used for boiling had to be destroyed. "But the earthen vessel wherein it is sodden shall be broken: and if it be sodden in a brasen pot, it shall be both scoured, and rinsed in water" (Lev. 6:28).

The Offerer's Portion—*Nothing.* This was the sin offering, and we are the guilty party. We can do nothing at all in the matter of our sin or its redemption. It is all of grace.

The Typical Teaching—*Christ is our Sin Offering.* The priest may sin, nations may fall into idolatry, rulers may lead people astray, individuals may fail and come short, for *all* have sinned and come short of the glory of God. Whoever, wherever, however, sin is sin; whether we call it small or large, black or white, justifiable or unjustifiable, intentional or unintentional, it makes no difference so far as God is concerned. It must be dealt with, and He Himself has made the complete and only provision, which is declared in the New Testament. "For what the law could not do, in that it was weak through the flesh, God sending his own Son in the likeness of sinful flesh, and for sin, condemned sin in the flesh" (Rom. 8:3).

To understand this verse, one or two questions must be asked—the first, what was it that the law could not do seeing the Psalmist says: "The law of the Lord is perfect, converting the soul" (Ps. 19:7)? The answer is given in Galatians 2:16: "Knowing that a man is not justified by the works of the law, but by the faith of Jesus Christ, even we have believed in Jesus Christ, that we might be justified by the faith of Christ, and not by the works of the law: for by the works of the law shall no flesh be justified." The law could not justify. It covered sin but was unable to remove the sin.

The second question would be, if the law were made weak through the flesh, then what flesh? It is generally assumed that this refers to the human flesh or our sinful flesh, but this interpretation does not fit into the text.

Human flesh cannot weaken a perfect or eternal law.

The law required that when a man sinned he should offer a bullock as a sin offering, but how could an animal take the place of a sinner and bring him deliverance from sin? Man is human, the bullock is animal. Man is a moral being, the animal is amoral. They are of two different natures. Man knows temptation, trial, failure, sin, but the animal knows none of these things. It has no moral standards, knows no law, has no sense of right and wrong; in other words, it does not possess my flesh, my nature, my morals. It is totally different in its being; therefore, how could it take my place and become my substitute? The answer is that it could not. So the law, with its demands, became weak or noneffective through the flesh of that animal. Therefore ". . . what the law could not do [justify] in that it was weak through the flesh [animal flesh], God sending his own Son in the likeness of sinful flesh [human flesh—Jesus becoming Man], and for sin, condemned sin in the flesh." "For he hath made him to be sin for us, who knew no sin; that we might be made the righteousness of God in him" (2 Cor. 5:21).

As in this offering sin passed from man to the sinless animal by the laying on of hands (imputation), after which the animal was slain (expiation), so by faith my sin passed from me, the sinful one, to Christ, the sinless One, causing Him to become (my) sin; then, when He died, my sin died in Him, and I live having been made the righteousness of God in Him.

A third New Testament scripture, bearing on this same subject, is: "We have an altar, whereof they have no right to eat which serve the tabernacle. For the bodies of those beasts, whose blood is brought into the sanctuary by the high priest for sin, are burned without the camp Wherefore Jesus also, that He might sanctify the people with His own blood, suffered without the gate. Let us go forth therefore unto Him without the camp, bearing His reproach" (Heb. 13:10–13).

Two things stand out prominently in these verses. The blood went in—the body went out. The body went outside the camp in judgment because sin was on it. The blood went in in reconciliation because God had accepted it. Outside, Christ met man's need; inside, Christ met God's demands, and so a reconciliation was made. If we are identified with Him in His suffering in the world today, we shall be welcomed together with Him in His glory by and by.

The Symbolism—*Atonement.* So far as we are concerned

> Jesus paid it all,
> All to Him I owe;
> Sin had left a crimson stain,
> He washed it white as snow.

Death has taken place, the price has been paid. We are free through expiation.

5

THE TRESPASS OFFERING

And he shall bring his trespass offering unto the Lord
for his sin which he hath sinned, a female from the flock,
a lamb or a kid of the goats, for a sin offering; and the
priest shall make an atonement for him concerning his
sin. And if he be not able to bring a lamb, then he shall
bring for his trespass, which he hath committed, two
turtledoves, or two young pigeons, unto the Lord; one
for a sin offering, and the other for a burnt offering (Lev.
5:6,7).

Likewise this is the law of the trespass offering: it is
most holy. In the place where they kill the burnt offering shall they kill the trespass offering: and the blood
thereof shall he sprinkle round about upon the altar.
And he shall offer of it all the fat thereof; the rump, and
the fat that covereth the inwards, and the two kidneys,
and the fat that is on them, which is by the flanks, and
the caul that is above the liver, with the kidneys, it shall
he take away: and the priest shall burn them upon the
altar for an offering made by fire unto the Lord: it is a
trespass offering. Every male among the priests shall eat
thereof: it shall be eaten in the holy place: it is most holy.
As the sin offering is, so is the trespass offering: there is
one law for them: the priest that maketh atonement
therewith shall have it. And the priest that offereth any
man's burnt offering, even the priest shall have to himself the skin of the burnt offering which he hath offered.
And all the meat offering that is baken in the oven, and

all that is dressed in the fryingpan, and in the pan, shall be the priest's that offereth it. And every meat offering, mingled with oil, and dry, shall all the sons of Aaron have, one as much as another (Lev. 7:1–10).

THE trespass offering will have to be approached differently from the others because, in this instance, the offering was

According to practice. It enlarged on a number of specific sins which were important enough to be listed by God, and so must be important enough to demand individual attention. One of the notable distinctions between the sin offering and the trespass offering is that, in the latter, restitution was always required. Of course, the trespass offering was in fact part of the sin offering. Sin is coming short of God's standards. Trespassing is overstepping the mark. It also means the unlawful possession of another's property. This is appreciated whenever the notice is seen "Trespassers will be prosecuted." A boundary line has to be crossed.

The Tresspass. (1) *Concealing truth.* "And if a soul sin, and hear the voice of swearing, and is a witness, whether he hath seen or known of it; if he do not utter it, then he shall bear his iniquity" (Lev. 5:1).

This swearing does not refer to blasphemy, but to the taking of an oath as in a law court. God demanded that judgment should be meted out to the law breaker. This was the punishment of the man committing crime, and thereby keeping crime checked, and also for the protection of the innocent person. In view of this divine command, any person who withholds evidence when it is demanded in the name of justice becomes a participant in the crime. This is known in British Law as "aiding and abetting," and is punishable. History is full of evidence to this fact. This is why in the law court a person is required to take an oath on the Bible to "declare the truth, the whole truth, and nothing but the truth." If we are to live honorably before God we must live honestly before men.

Two examples of this law, from the Old and New Testaments, one negative and the other positive, would prove of great interest. When Joshua destroyed the city of Jericho and then moved on to the smaller town of Ai, the Israelites were defeated. The reason was made known that sin was in the camp. Achan had stolen of the spoils of Jericho which should have been dedicated to the Lord. When it was discovered, he and his sons and daughters were stoned to death. It has been a problem in many minds as to why his family should have died because of the sin of the father. The inference is that the family was aware of the sin and had not made it known, so when by a process of elimination Achan was discovered, the children were participants in the sin by their silence.

The more outstanding and positive illustration comes from the life of the Lord. Jesus was standing before the false witnesses who lay against Him every kind of accusation, to which the Lord made no response. This angered the high priest so that he cried: "Answerest thou nothing? What is it which these witness against thee? But Jesus held his peace" (Matt. 26:62,63). The Lord was certainly fulfilling the prophecy Isaiah had made concerning Him: "He was oppressed, and he was afflicted, yet he opened not his mouth: he is brought as a lamb to the slaughter, and as a sheep before her shearers is dumb, so he openeth not his mouth" (Isa. 53:7).

Caiaphas, indignant with his "prisoner," and as high priest fully acquainted with the law, made use of Lev 5:1, when he said: "I adjure [swear] thee by the living God, that thou tell us whether thou be the Christ, the Son of God" (Matt. 26:63). Jesus had now heard the voice of swearing. If, at that moment, He had failed to answer, He would have committed a sin, become a sinner, and failed to become man's Redeemer. However, Jesus was as fully cognizant of the law as was Caiaphas, and replied: "Thou has said; . . ." (Matt. 26:64), and thereby remained sinless.

A Christian has to live as consistently as this every day.

(2) *Defilement.* "Or if a soul touch any unclean thing, . . . or if he touch the uncleanness of man . . . when he knoweth of it, then he shall be guilty" (Lev. 5:2,3).

This sounds to be a very severe law, but one has to remember that the children of Israel were surrounded by nations all of whom were given to idolatry, and God was concerned that His people should keep themselves from being contaminated, not merely with that which would defile the body, but also the soul. God was seeking to reach the spiritual life of His people through the medium of material things. A dead body or a leprous person would defile one who contacted it, as in the present days there are certain diseases which are know to be contagious, and therefore every precaution is taken to avoid such. The Lord would teach us to shun as sin every form of impurity, whether it be in book, or conversation, or acquaintance, for such things can defile the soul and damage the spriritual life. Even if one does these things in ignorance and learns of it later, he is guilty.

(3) *Swearing rashly.* "Or if a soul swear, pronouncing with his lips to do evil, or to do good, whatsoever it be that a man shall pronounce with an oath, and it be hid from him; when he knoweth of it, then he shall be guilty in one of these" (Lev. 5:4).

This is very different from the act of swearing under oath. It is related to making promises, entering into contracts, or making vows.

On reading the verse, again it would appear that there is an outstanding injustice, if not a contradiction. It is understandable that if a person declared that he would perform some good thing and then failed to do it, he would be in the wrong, but if a person declared that he was going to carry out some evil project and then repented of his intent, that act would be justifiable; but the text says No! He is still a guilty man.

This is a matter of emphasis. The verse is not concerned with the good or the evil; it is concerned with the oath. It is a demand for care in the form of our speech which can quickly cause us to fall into sin. Our promises to do good or evil must not be rash, and they must never be taken in the name of the Lord. So often people promise to give money, maintain a missionary, give this or do that, in the name of the Lord. Often one is asked to sign a covenant of some kind—"I promise by the help of God." This is the thing that the Lord does not permit because "Thou shalt not take the name of the Lord thy God in vain; for the Lord will not hold him guiltless that taketh his name in vain" (Exod. 20: 7). To promise anything in the name of the Lord and then fail in its fulfillment is to take His name in vain. It is "swearing rashly." Never bring that holy name of the Lord into the affairs of life, unless you are determined that at *all* costs you will fulfill that commitment.

Here is what the Word of the Lord has to say about it: "Again, ye have heard that it hath been said by them of old time, Thou shalt not forswear thyself, but shalt perform unto the Lord thine oaths: but I say unto you, *Swear not at all*; neither by heaven; for it is God's throne: nor by the earth; for it is His footstool: neither by Jerusalem; for it is the city of the great King. Neither shalt thou swear by thy head, because thou canst not make one hair white or black. But let your communication be, Yea, yea; Nay, nay: for whatsoever is more than these cometh of evil" (Matt. 5: 33–37). "But above all things, my brethren, *swear not*, neither by heaven, neither by the earth, neither by any other oath: but let your yea be yea; and your nay, nay; lest ye fall into condemnation" (James 5: 12). Therefore, in all promises just be satisfied with yes or no.

The psalmist meant the same thing when he said: "Set a watch, O Lord, before my mouth; keep the door of my lips" (Ps. 14:3).

Jacob, at the time when he fled from Esau his brother, was met by God at Bethel. In his alarm "Jacob vowed a vow, saying, If God will be with me, and will keep me in this way that I go, and will give me bread to eat, and raiment to put on, so that I come again to my father's house in peace; then shall the Lord be my God: and this stone, which I have set for a pillar, shall be God's house: and of all that thou shalt give me I will surely give the tenth unto thee" (Gen. 28:20–22).

God, who often referred to Himself as "the God of Abraham, of Isaac, and of Jacob," appeared to Jacob and said: "I am the God of Bethel, where thou anointedst the pillar, and where thou *vowedst a vow* unto Me: now arise, get thee out from his land, and return unto the land of thy kindred" (Gen. 31:13).

Many people are perplexed concerning the story of Jephthah, and cannot accept that he offered his daughter as a sacrifice. Therefore they seek to explain that she lived a life of virginity, their reasoning being that God did not permit human sacrifice. This is true, but neither does God allow His name to be taken in vain. The heart of the story is: "And Jephthah *vowed a vow* unto the Lord, and said, If Thou shalt without fail deliver the children of Ammon into my hands, then . . . I will offer it up for a burnt offering" (Read Judges 11:29–40). Better to offer a human sacrifice than profane the name of a holy God.

All this is borne out by yet another scripture: "If a man vow a vow unto the Lord, or swear an oath to bind his soul with a bond; he shall not break his word, he shall do according to all that proceedeth out of his mouth. If a woman also vow a vow unto the Lord, and bind herself by a bond, being in her father's house in her youth; and her father hear her vow, and her bond wherewith she hath bound her soul, and her father shall hold his peace at her: then all her vows shall stand, and every bond wherewith she hath bound her soul shall stand" (Num. 30:2-4).

Humbleness and gentleness are the safest paths of life, letting our yea be yea, and our nay, nay—which mean yes or no, without the addition of oaths and promises which become committals that bind. God binds the man who binds himself with an oath.

Special note must be made of the fact that if the oath were *good* and man failed to fulfill it, he was guilty and must offer a trespass offering. If a man swore to do evil and he did not do it, he sinned. This man was in a dilemma. If he did the thing he declared, he sinned. If he did not commit the thing, he still sinned and must offer his trespass offering, which means that in the mind of God breaking a vow is more grievous than fulfilling an evil intent, so the lesser must be done because of the import of the greater. In the light of this, let us pray: "Lord, guard Thou the words of my lips."

(4) *Dishonesty in holy things.* "If a soul commit a trespass, and sin through ignorance, in the holy things of the Lord; then he shall bring for his trespass unto the Lord a ram without blemish out of the flocks, with thy estimation by shekels of silver, after the shekel of the sanctuary, for a trespass offering: and he shall make amends for the harm that he hath done in the holy thing, and shall add the fifth part thereto, and give it unto the priest: and the priest shall make an atonement for him with the ram of the trespass offering, and it shall be forgiven him" (Lev. 5:15,16).

Dishonesty is twofold. It can be against God, or it can be against man. In these immediate verses, and in those that follow concerning ignorance, the sins were against God. The remaining details of the trespass offering were sins against man.

Man might be as free today as he was in the days of Malachi to ask if it were possible for a man to rob God, and the answer would still be the same—yes, even though it might be through ignorance in his understanding of holy things.

It is to be remembered that everything belongs to God, and man, too, belongs to Him, for He is the creator and the sustainer of all things. He is the sovereign ruler of the earth. "All things were made by him; and without him was not anything made that was made" (John 1:3).

God claimed for Himself the firstborn of man and beast (Exod. 13:2).

God claimed half a shekel per head ransom money from every man who joined the army of Israel (Exod. 30: 11–16).

God claimed the firstfruits of the harvest (Lev. 23: 10–14).

God claimed tithes of all man possessed—and that would include time, energy, service, as well as possessions (Lev. 27:30–32).

When God gave to Israel the land of promise, as they entered into its conquest under the leadership of Joshua, He required that the first city, Jericho, should be dedicated to Himself by fire (Joshua 6).

In the New Testament He has claimed much more because He has given to man much more. He gave Himself; He asks that we should give ourselves; but man has ever been slow to give to God the things He requests—yea, more: the things He demands. To withhold is to rob. "Will a man rob God? Yet ye have robbed me. But ye say, wherein have we robbed Thee? In tithes and offerings" (Mal. 3:8). It may be unintentional, but that does not alter his responsibility.

God is robbed when we fail to give Him that one day in seven for worship and quiet meditation. He has given us six days and asks that we should give Him one. Is He asking too much? As a nation we have robbed Him of that day and can no longer expect His blessing; but how about ourselves as individuals?

God is robbed in our defective liberality. "Bring ye all the tithes into the storehouse" (Mal. 3:10). God is robbed in our lack of responsibility toward the Christian ministry, for He has declared that a laborer is worthy of his hire. God is robbed in our failure to maintain His work. The church is yielding ground everywhere because of lack of support financially and practically. We are not supporting God's church by our presence at the meetings, by our prayers for the ministry, by our interest in the missionary programme, by our personal invitation to others, as it ought to be supported. God is robbed of the worship which is due to His holy name. He is robbed when we neglect His Word. What is done today amounts to a constant asking of favors from God and never giving worship to God.

Are we honest with our time, our possessions, our abilities, our privileges, our responsibilities, our friends?

This dishonesty in holy things is a trespass for which God requires amends and restoration.

(5) *Ignorance.* "And if a soul sin, and commit any of these things which are forbidden to be done by the commandments of the Lord; though he wist it not, yet is he guilty, and shall bear his iniquity" (Lev. 5:17).

The sin of ignorance is not only stated in the above verse but is repeated a number of times in the chapter in the words "though he wist it not." On first reading this would appear to be another injustice, but on second reading, or upon consideration, one would realize that it is not so. The natural man reasons that if he is ignorant, how can be be responsible?

The author remembers reasoning with the police on one occasion, when his car had been impounded because, ignorantly, it had been parked in a non-parking area. All the pleading of innocence was of no avail. Sin, known or unknown, is a departure from the right. ". . . where no law is, there is no transgression" (Rom. 4:15). But we are not without law. The problem was that the police had set up a signpost intimating the new law, but it had not been seen because of an obstruction. Although innocent, the law had still been broken and so guilt was established.

The question would be, Why are we ignorant? Is the claim of ignorance just? Much of what we claim to be ignorance is willful, and therefore is sin. If a local authority provides motorists with a manual of rules and conduct on the high road, and the motorist refuses or does not bother to read the manual, can he claim ignorance? The law says No. Such a person is punishable, and the rest of society would agree.

God has provided mankind with a manual of laws and conduct—the Bible. In it God has laid down His laws. He has set forth the whole code of a moral life, and all the principles of a spiritual life. He has declared the punishments that must be meted out for disobedience, and the rewards for obedience. If a man refuses to read the Bible to find the mind of Christ, or having read it he fails to accept its revelation, or satisfies himself with his own interpretation of that law, accepting this and rejecting that, then he becomes guilty in the eyes of God. This man is definitely willful. If a man could find out but does not, he is guilty. Needless forgetfulness is also sin. This is not ignorance; it is the sin of ignorance.

Blunting spiritual perception is willful ignorance Measuring conduct by our own standards is willful.

If the Jews had read their law with an open mind, they would have known their Messiah. Then they would not have crucified the Lord of glory. If one does not know, then it becomes his duty to find out.

The next trespasses were not against God but against fellow men.

(6) *Failure in our trust.* "If a soul sin, and commit a trespass against the Lord, and lie unto his neighbour in that which was delivered him to keep . . ." (Lev. 6:2).

If one accepts another person's property or possessions, with the promise to protect or safeguard them, he becomes morally responsible to fulfill the promise, and in due time to return to the owner that which has been in his custody. To accept the possession with an ulterior motive, or to fail to secure it so that it cannot be lost or stolen, is the "lie." To make an excuse to the owner to deliver oneself from the responsibility accepted is also the "lie." The lesson to learn here is that we are responsible people, and that every commitment of life is very important. Again it is the matter of honesty. In 2 Kings 6:5 it is recorded: "But as one was felling a beam, the axe head fell into the water: and he cried, and said, Alas, Master! for it was borrowed." The concern was that the axe was not his, it was borrowed. Man must be concerned about borrowed goods, and more concerned about entrusted goods. May the Lord deliver us from carelessness at any time, because we will be held responsible for such conduct and will have to make amends—such is trespassing.

(7) *Unfairness in partnership.* "If a soul sin, and commit a trespass against the Lord . . . in fellowship" (Lev. 6:2).

In the margin the word "fellowship" is translated "bargain." The idea is one of partnership. The Lord is showing what His mind is concerning our everyday behavior as people who are in the world but not of it. How do we relate to other people? Is that relationship such as becomes the gospel of Jesus Christ and our Christian profession?

This partnership not only operates in the business world, where we are not to be unequally yoked with unbelievers, but it applies in all ways and in all things where another person is involved. It is doing the fair share, not acting as top dog and taking the choice parts, always being the leader and letting the other person do the dirty work or carry the heavy load. This applies in business, in the home, in the church, in our social life, everywhere —always playing a fair game.

(8) *Taking by violence.* "If a soul sin, and commit a trespass against the Lord, . . . in a thing taken away by violence" (Lev. 6:2).

This statement is not limited to open assault, hitting and robbing the other man on the highway. A Christian would not even think of doing such a thing. It is that the other man has a will, and that will is as much his as is his money or any other material possession. Every man has a right to think. He is entitled to make his own decisions and conduct himself as his conscience permits.

There are strong-willed, determined men who insist on having their own way and exercising their authority, or their thinking, irrespective of whether the other person agrees, or whether his conscience is hurt or offended. This is taking the other man's personality and mind from him by violence. The dictionary says, among other things, that violence is "any unjust or unwarranted exertion of force or power, as against rights, laws, etc." As Christians we need to learn to respect the other person's rights and privileges. We may seek to persuade a person to change his point of view, but never force him. We must learn to agree, or to agree to differ.

(9) *Deception.* "If a soul sin, and commit a trespass against the Lord . . . or hath deceived his neighbour" (Lev. 6:2).

This means to obtain under false pretenses. The Bible is full of records of deception and the consequences. Jacob deceived Esau, the Gibeonites deceived Joshua, Delilah deceived Samson, Ananias and Sapphira sought to deceive Peter. Today children deceive their parents and teachers, workmen deceive their masters, and masters their work-people. Even Christians deceive each other, and many of us try to deceive God. In the sight of God these are trespasses upon each other for which we will be held responsible, and for which God demands amends.

(10) *Keeping things found.* "If a soul sin, and commit a trespass against the Lord, . . . or have found that which was lost, and lieth concerning it, and sweareth falsely" (Lev.6:2,3).

This is a dishonesty. As Christians it is our duty to do all that is within our power to discover the owner of anything we may find, and see that it is duly returned. "Finders, keepers" is a worldly attitude that is both selfish and wrong. The Lord has always required absolute honesty.

Throughout there is the reminder that if we take care of the little things of our conduct, then the big things will take care of themselves; also there is that potent truth that the Lord does not close His eyes to the little things which we treat so carelessly.

Having detailed the practices, the ritual of this trespass offering must now be considered.

The Nature of the Offering—*According to practice. Lamb, goat, turtledoves, pigeons, fine flour.* In the first three failures, the offering was a female lamb or a kid of the goats, or two turtledoves or two young pigeons, all of them in the prime of life. This offering included a sin offering and a burnt offering. Some scholars consider that the first fifteen verses of chapter five are still the sin offering. It is a little difficult to discern because, on the one hand, the word trespass is used, while, on the other hand, part of the sin offering was required. However, there was the alternative of the tenth part of an ephah of fine flour that could be offered, and this would not have met the requirements of the sin offering.

In the rest of the failures the situation is a little clearer. A ram was included, plus an estimation, plus a fine equal to a double tithe—two-tenths or one-fifth. When the trespass was against man there was the restoration of the principal, plus a fifth, to the owner, and a ram, with a fine, to the priest.

One of the major differences between the sin offering and the trespass offering was that in the latter restitution was always required.

The Offerer's Work—*Confession.* "And it shall be, when he shall be guilty in one of these things, that he shall confess that he hath sinned in that thing" (Lev. 5:5). "Then it shall be, because he hath sinned, and is guilty, that . . . he shall even restore it in the principal, and shall add the fifth part more thereto, and give it unto him to whom it appertaineth, in the day of his trespass offering" (Lev. 6:4,5).

First, the offerer had to make confession *"in that thing."* This was not a general confession which could be an easy ritualistic citation. It was a personal, particular confession of a specific sin committed. This brought about a deep sense of guilt, followed by humiliation. He must obtain forgiveness and must make restitution, plus that which again emphasized guilt, thus making sin and carelessness to be unprofitable things.

Present-day crime could be greatly eliminated, and innocent people protected, if our prevailing laws were based upon those laid down by God, so that crime became expensive to the criminal instead of lucrative.

The Priest's Work—*Sprinkling blood.* In the matter of the first three trespasses, the blood of the first bird was sprinkled on the side of the altar, and the remainder of the blood poured out at the bottom of the altar. The second bird was used as a burnt offering. In the event of the offering being one of fine flour, a handful was burned by the priest as it was given to God. In the remaining trespasses, the blood of the ram was sprinkled round the altar, as in the sin offering—without the shedding of blood there is no remission.

God's Portion—*All that was burned.* This was the rump and all the internal fat. The fat was the best because of its significance—see God's portion of the peace offering.

The Priest's Portion—*The remainder.* That which was not offered to God by fire. The portion which went to God was always a memorial—that which represented and was accepted as the whole. The servants of God are sharers in the blessings of God.

The Offerer's Portion—*Nothing.* He was the offender and was meeting the requirements of the law, and as an offender he had no merits.

The Typical Teaching—*Christ our Trespass Offering.* "For the transgression of my people was He stricken" (Isa. 53:8).

Christ has given Himself, the one offering for sin, and He died. We are all debtors to God, having trespassed against Him; but as we are unable to pay the penalty required by law, He became the lamb, the goat, the turtledove, the young pigeon, even the fine flour, and so has made full provision. Hence the claims of God were not avoided, but justly met in Him who was our Trespass Offering. "To wit, that God was in Christ, reconciling the world unto himself, not imputing their trespasses unto them; and hath committed unto us the word of reconciliation" (2 Cor. 5:19). "And you, being dead in your sins and the uncircumcision of your flesh, hath He quickened together with him, having forgiven you all trespasses; blotting out the handwriting of ordinances that was against us, which was contrary to us, and took it out of the way, nailing it to his cross" (Col. 2:13,14).

Symbolism—*Restoration*. While the Lord has made full provision for us with the Father, we have certain commitments and responsibilities here on earth. The trespasser had in each instance to make amends, restoring all his wrongful gains. Lest some might want to see something meritorious in making good, a confession had to be made of the wrong he had done, and a sacrifice had to go with it as a token of complete unworthiness.

6

THE PEACE OFFERING

And if his oblation be a sacrifice of peace offering, if
he offer it of the herd; whether it be a male or female, he
shall offer it without blemish before the Lord. And he
shall lay his hand upon the head of his offering, and kill it
at the door of the tabernacle of the congregation: and
Aaron's sons the priests shall sprinkle the blood upon
the altar round about. And he shall offer of the sacrifice
of the peace offering an offering made by fire unto the
Lord; the fat that covereth the inwards, and all the fat
that is upon the inwards, and the two kidneys, and the
fat that is on them, which is by the flanks, and the caul
above the liver, with the kidneys, it shall he take away.
And Aaron's sons shall burn it on the altar upon the
burnt sacrifice, which is upon the wood that is on the
fire: it is an offering made by fire, of a sweet savour unto
the Lord. And if his offering for a sacrifice of peace
offering unto the Lord be of the flock; male or female,
he shall offer it without blemish. If he offer a lamb for
his offering, then shall he offer it before the Lord. And
he shall lay his hand upon the head of his offering, and
kill it before the tabernacle of the congregation: and
Aaron's sons shall sprinkle the blood thereof round
about upon the altar. And he shall offer of the sacrifice
of the peace offering an offering made by fire unto the
Lord; the fat thereof, and the whole rump, it shall he
take off hard by the backbone; and the fat that covereth
the inwards, and all the fat that is upon the inwards, and

the two kidneys, and the fat that is upon them, which is by the flanks, and the caul above the liver, with the kidneys, it shall he take away. And the priest shall burn it upon the altar: it is the food of the offering made by fire unto the Lord. And if his offering be a goat, then he shall offer it before the Lord. And he shall lay his hand upon the head of it, and kill it before the tabernacle of the congregation: and the sons of Aaron shall sprinkle the blood thereof upon the altar round about. And he shall offer thereof his offering, even an offering made by fire unto the Lord; the fat that covereth the inwards, and all the fat that is upon the inwards, and the two kidneys, and the fat that is upon them, which is by the flanks, and the caul above the liver, with the kidneys, it shall he take away. And the priest shall burn them upon the altar: it is the food of the offering made by fire for a sweet savour: all the fat is the Lord's. It shall be a perpetual statute for your generations throughout all your dwellings, that ye eat neither fat nor blood (Lev. 3:1–17).

And this is the law of the sacrifice of peace offerings, which he shall offer unto the Lord. If he offer it for a thanksgiving, then he shall offer with the sacrifice of thanksgiving unleavened cakes mingled with oil, and unleavened wafers anointed with oil, and cakes mingled with oil, of fine flour, fried. Besides the cakes, he shall offer for his offering leavened bread with the sacrifice of thanksgiving of his peace offerings. And of it he shall offer one out of the whole oblation for an heave offering unto the Lord, and it shall be the priest's that sprinkleth the blood of the peace offerings. And the flesh of the sacrifice of his peace offerings for thanksgiving shall be eaten the same day that it is offered; he shall not leave any of it until the morning. But if the sacrifice of his offering be a vow, or a voluntary offering, it shall be eaten the same day that he offereth his sacrifice: and on the morrow also the remainder of it shall be eaten: but the remainder of the flesh of the sacrifice on the third day shall be burnt with fire. And if any of the flesh of the sacrifice of his peace offerings be eaten at all on the third day, it shall not be accepted, neither shall it be imputed unto him that offereth it: it shall be an abomination, and the soul that eateth of it shall bear his iniquity. And the flesh that toucheth any unclean thing shall not be eaten; it shall be burnt with fire: and as for the flesh, all that be clean shall eat thereof. But the soul that eateth of the flesh of the sacrifice of peace offerings, that pertain unto the Lord, having his uncleanness upon him, even that soul shall be cut off from his people. Moreover the soul that shall touch any unclean thing, as the uncleanness of man, or any unclean beast, or any abominable unclean thing, and eat of the flesh of the sacrifice of peace offerings, which pertain unto the Lord, even that soul shall be cut off from his people (Lev. 7:11–21).

As already pointed out, although the peace offering was third in the order set out in these early chapters of Leviticus, it was the last in the order of observance. In that place it is now to be considered. It was last in observance because peace comes to the soul as a result of complying with all that God has required.

Dr. J. A. Seiss points out that "The word *peace,* in the language of the Scriptures, has a shade of meaning not commonly attached to it in ordinary use. With most persons it signifies a cessation of hostilities, harmonious agreement, tranquillity, the absence of disturbance. But in the Scripture it means more. Its predominant import there is, *prosperity, welfare, joy, happiness.* The original Hebrew word includes both of these meanings" (*The Gospel in Leviticus,* p. 64).

This, then, was a gathering together of the priests and the people with their God to feast joyously in all the wonderful things that the Lord had done for them. It was a wonderful culmination of all that had transpired. As we consider it may the same rejoicing be our experience.

Nature of the Offering—*Common to all. Bullock, lamb, or goat.* Each of these animals, which had to be without blemish, would be characteristic of Christ in His perfect life upon earth.

The ox represented the Lord as the strong and patient One.

The lamb represented the Lord as the meek and gentle One.

The goat represented the Lord as the despised and rejected One.

While much of the book of Leviticus appears to be repetition, in fact it is not. The detail becomes part of the fascination of its study. Whereas in the other four offerings there was a variation of requirement according to the offerer, viz: according to possessions, according to property, according to position, and according to practice, in the peace offering there was no distinction at all. This offering was common to all.

What is to be noted in the peace offering is the difference in

(1) *The Victims.* While in some of the offerings there were birds, these were not acceptable in the peace offering. Two reasons would account for this. In the first place, fat was an important essential because it was to be God's portion, but there was a lack of fat in the birds which could not meet the demand. Secondly, the peace offering was the only one to be shared by three parties. The birds would not be large enough for this division.

(2) *The Sexes.* The animals could be male or female. In other instances only the male was required. The male and female is the greatest symbol of friendship. A friendship which had not existed between God and man owing to sin had now been established, because through the earlier offerings sin had been removed, and now God and man were brought together in a oneness. They were feasting

together and fellowshipping together in a joyous celebration.

(3) *The Treatment.* The burnt offering was a whole burnt offering. All of it was for God. In the peace offering only the fat was offered to God. God and priest and offerer, all shared the blessings now complete.

While there were these differences, there were also similarities. All had to be without blemish. Where an animal was concerned, there was identification with its death and an application of the blood, for without the shedding of blood there was no remission. It is the blood which has opened a new and living way to God, and by it we have salvation and peace.

The Offerer's Work—*Slay the offering.* "And he shall lay his hand upon the head of his offering, and kill it at the door of the tabernacle of the congregation" (Lev. 3:2).

The offerer had to lead the offering to the door of the tabernacle, lay his hands upon the head of it as an act of identification, kill it, take out the fat around the caul and the kidneys and give it to the priest to be burned. That was all. Man only has to be obedient and give to God that which is His due; that is, never give Him the leftovers or the part we can do without, but always the very best, the firstfruits. We shall see presently how important this is.

The Priest's Work—*Wave breast and shoulder.* The priest took the blood of the sacrifice and sprinkled it around the altar, after which he burned the fat upon the altar, ". . . the fat that covereth the inwards, and all the fat that is upon the inwards, and the two kidneys, and the fat that is on them, which is by the flanks, and the caul above the liver, with the kidneys, it shall he take away. And Aaron's sons shall burn it on the altar . . ." (Lev. 3:3–5). He then had to present the breast and right shoulder to the Lord. ". . . He that offereth the sacrifice of his peace offerings unto the Lord shall bring his oblation unto the Lord of the sacrifice

of his peace offerings. His own hands shall bring the
offerings of the Lord made by fire, the fat with the breast,
it shall he bring, that the breast may be waved for a wave
offering before the Lord. And the priest shall burn the fat
upon the altar . . ." (Lev. 7:29–31).

The breast denoted affection and the shoulder represented strength. These should be yielded to the Lord.
The priest, having presented these to the Lord, received
them back from the Lord, as we receive back with interest
all that we dedicate to Him and to His service.

God's Portion—*The fat and the inwards.* "And he shall
offer thereof his offering, even an offering made by fire
unto the Lord; the fat that covereth the inwards, and all the
fat that is upon the inwards, and the two kidneys, and the
fat that is upon them, which is by the flanks, and the caul
above the liver, with the kidneys, it shall he take away.
And the priest shall burn them upon the altar: it is the food
of the offering made by fire for a sweet savour: all the fat is
the Lord's" (Lev. 3:14–16).

This was the fat of the inwards, which is called suet, and
not the fat that runs in the lean. It was considered the best
part of the beast and was loved by the Easterner. It was
required by God. Quoting from the British Encyclopedia
fat is "an animal substitute of a more or less oily character,
deposited in vessels, in tissues. It forms a considerable
layer under the skin, is collected in large quantity around
certain organs, as for instance, the kidneys, fills up furrows
on the surface of the heart, surrounds joints, and exists in
large quantities in the marrow of bones. It is an excellent
packing material in the body, being light, soft, and elastic.
Being a bad conductor of heat, it enables a person to retain
the warmth he has generated, but its chief use is for the
purpose of nutrition."

Fat is, therefore, that which protects the vital life-giving,
health-sustaining parts of the body, keeps the warmth, and

feeds every part of the being. That is what the Lord required—all that maintains spiritual life, keeps the warmth and love of our devotion, and feeds the soul with divine energy and a spiritual fervor.

Added to the fat of the inwards, God had another requirement concerning the lambs. "And he shall offer of the sacrifice of the peace offering an offering made by fire unto the Lord; the fat thereof, and the whole rump, it shall he take off hard by the backbone . . ." (Lev. 3:9). The literal rendering is "the whole tail cut off hard by the backbone." There is a breed of sheep in the East which grows a long and heavy tail, weighing upwards to twenty pounds, most of which is fat. This part of the animal is considered sweet and valuable, and is greatly appreciated by the Easterner. They loved this fat so much that if they could, they would keep part of the tail for themselves; hence the statements that the tail should be "cut off hard by the backbone," and "all the fat is the Lord's."

Fat burns very quickly and fiercely. This would suggest the readiness of the Lord to accept the best when it is offered to Him. When things are accepted by God they become sacred, and must no longer be treated as ordinary things. "Speak unto the children of Israel, saying, Ye shall eat no manner of fat, of ox, or of sheep, or of goat. . . . For whosoever eateth the fat of the beast, of which men offer an offering made by fire unto the Lord, even the soul that eateth it shall be cut off from his people" (Lev. 7:23,25).

The Priest's Portion—*Breast and shoulder.* This was the wave breast and the heave shoulder. There is a point of interest in the allocation of these portions. The breast is the symbol of affection. It went to the priesthood and was shared by the whole family, as the love and affection of the Lord is shared by all His children. The shoulder is the symbol of strength. This was for the particular priest who offered the particular sacrifice, a reminder that the strength of the Lord is given to those who serve.

The Offerer's Portion—*The remainder.* It was the only offering in which the offerer had a share. All that was left, after the Lord had received the fat and the priest had received the breast and right shoulder, was eaten by him and his friends in the court of the tabernacle. They were rejoicing in the finished work of their God.

The Typical Teaching—*Christ our Peace Offering.* Peace was declared when Christ was born. Said the angels: "Glory to God in the highest, and on earth *peace,* goodwill toward men" (Luke 2:14).

Peace was manifested in Christ's ministry: "Therefore being justified by faith, we have *peace* with God through our Lord Jesus Christ" (Rom 5:1).

Peace was secured through His death: "And having made *peace* through the blood of his cross, by him to reconcile all things unto himself; by him, I say, whether they be things in earth, or things in heaven" (Col. 1:20).

Peace is ours through believing: "For He is our *peace* [offering], who hath made both one, and hath broken down the middle wall of partition between us" (Eph. 2:14).

The Symbolism—*Reconciliation.* Through all that Christ has accomplished upon the cross, through that one great sacrifice which was made once in the end of the age, He has perfected for us a complete reconciliation. We recognize and accept ". . . that God was in Christ, reconciling the world unto himself, not imputing their trespasses unto them; and hath committed unto us the word of reconciliation" (2 Cor. 5:19).

The peace offering ended in a joyous feasting together of priests and people with their God in the court of the tabernacle. This is intimated in Deuteronomy 12:5-7: "But unto the place which the Lord your God shall choose out of all your tribes to put his name there, even unto his habitation shall ye seek, and thither thou shalt come: and thither ye shall bring your burnt offerings, and your sacrifices, and your tithes, and heave offerings of your hand, and your vows, and your freewill offerings, and the firstlings of your herds and of your flocks: and there ye shall eat before the Lord your God, and ye shall rejoice in all ye put your hand unto, ye and your households, wherein the Lord thy God hath blessed thee." "Thou mayest not eat within thy gates the tithe of thy corn, or of thy wine, or of thy oil, or the firstlings of thy herds or of thy flock, nor any of thy vows which thou vowest, nor thy freewill offerings, or heave offering of thine hand: but thou must eat them before the Lord thy God in the place which the Lord thy God shall choose, thou, and thy son, and thy daughter, and thy manservant, and thy maidservant, and the Levite that is within thy gates: and thou shalt rejoice before the Lord thy God in all that thou puttest thine hands unto" (Deut. 12: 17,18).

This feasting together in the fellowship of what has been accomplished by Christ, this *peace* which has been made sacred by the blood of His cross, this fellowship of believers, must be celebrated in the sanctity of the church as it was then celebrated within the court of the tabernacle.

There is much service to be rendered for the Lord in the world. There is a testimony to be borne to unbelievers. There is the day by day Christian living, but there is also the spiritual feasting with the Lord and with the saints, feasting on His Word, which must be done in the place where He shall choose to put His name. Did not Paul refer to this when he said: "Not forsaking the assembling of ourselves together, as the manner of some is" (Heb. 10: 25)?

Christ, having died, now lives, and we live in Him, feasting with Him, and sharing with others the peace of God which passeth all understanding.

SUMMARY

The burnt offering was according to possession.
The meal offering was according to property.
The sin offering was according to position.
The trespass offering was according to practice.
The peace offering was common to all.

The burnt offering was Consecration of Self.
The meal offering was Consecration of Gifts.
The sin offering was Atonement.
The trespass offering was Restoration.
The peace offering was Reconciliation.

The burnt offering was Christ our
   Passover .... Eph. 5:2.
The meal offering was Christ the
   Corn of Wheat .... John 12:24.
The sin offering was Christ our Sin
   Offering .... 2 Cor. 5:21.
The trespass offering was Christ our
   Trespass Offering .... Col. 2:13,14.
The peace offering was Christ our
   Peace Offering .... Eph. 2:14.

PART II

YOUR REASONABLE SERVICE

OR

THE FEASTS OF THE LORD

1

INTRODUCTION

THE book of Leviticus deals primarily with the worship of the people of God in the days prior to Christ's advent into this world. This worship was ordained by God, and made known to man by divine revelation. While the details are practical and were given for man's observation, at the same time they were typical, and were a pre-figuring of the claims of God and the worship of His people in the day of grace which would be after the advent of the Son of God. In this study both periods will be considered.

It has been pointed out in another book that the plan of Leviticus reveals God's great demand for holiness and His provision for it. This plan divides into two major sections, the first being the way to God through sacrifice. This has been considered in Part I in the five offerings, which have led man into a relationship with God wherein his sins have been dealt with and he is enjoying fellowship because of a peace that exists between God and man.

The second section is the walk with God through separation. Salvation is an act. Christianity is living Christ from day to day, walking with Him in a life of obedience. There are seven steps in this walk, and they are pictorialized in seven feasts known as the "Feasts of Jehovah." While the details of these feasts are to be found here and there, all seven are catalogued in the twenty-third chapter of Leviticus.

They are called the feasts of the Lord because He appointed them. God not only requested these feasts, but He also designated the time of the year when they should be observed—March, May, and September, according to our calendar. They were set at seasons when it would be easy to travel, and also between the busy times of the year so far as an agricultural people were concerned. The Lord has no desire to make spiritual life a burden; He desires that it should be a joyful experience. It is we who make it burdensome in ever wanting to put selfish desires first.

The seven feasts were observed by all the males of Israel over a period of seven months. Although there were seven feasts yet sometimes reference is made to three feasts. This is due to the fact that the feasts were so spaced that three trips to Jerusalem were sufficient for the observance of all seven. "Thrice in the year shall all your menchildren appear before the Lord God, the God of Israel" (Exod. 34: 23).

On their first journey to the capital city, which was in the first month of the year, three feasts were celebrated, the feast of Passover on the evening of the fourteenth day, the feast of unleavened bread from the fifteenth day lasting for a whole week, and the feast of firstfruits on the sixteenth day. This group was known as Passover, and became the first of the three journeys in which the people were involved.

A second journey was required seven weeks later for the observance of the feast of Pentecost, which was on the sixteenth day of the third month. This feast was on its own. The remaining group of three feasts, known as Tabernacles, required a third journey to the city. They were kept in the seventh month, the feast of trumpets on the first day of the month, the Day of Atonement on the tenth day, and the feast of tabernacles from the fifteenth until the twenty-second day.

The sequence of these feasts is very significant, revealing a divine plan and stamping the Bible with the seal of divine authority. The sequence not only reveals itself in the order of the feasts but it is manifested in the development of the Christian walk in the New Testament. The following study is set out in such a way as to reveal a threefold purpose:

(1) *The feast,* with all the ritual that belonged to the Old Testament days. This was set out by God, not merely for local observance but to be types, or pictures, setting forth other important truths. A type always anticipates.

(2) *An antitype,* or the New Testament fulfillment of the Old Testament symbol.

(3) *A spiritual application,* the same truths conveyed to the present day and applied to the progress of the Christian life.

Added to the seven annual feasts there were also the sabbaths. These, too, were feasts. There were the weekly sabbaths, and a number of special sabbaths, which were all religious feasts. These were not seasons of feasting in relationship to food (in fact, one of them was a fast), but they were festive occasions during which the people forsook the everyday pursuits of life for a season of rejoicing in the Lord's goodness to them. They were called convocations. Today they would be referred to as conventions, when the people of the Lord meet together in fellowship with each other, and feast together in the exposition of His Word and the other spiritual blessings that are shared.

They were all seasons of rest. The repeated declaration was: "Thou shalt do no servile work." In the case of the weekly sabbath the Lord said: "Six days shall work be done: but the seventh day is the sabbath of rest, an holy convocation; ye shall do no work therein: it is the sabbath of the Lord in all your dwellings" (Lev. 23: 3), meaning that it was a day free from work absolutely and entirely. "In all your dwellings" means in all parts of the land, in the home, hamlet, village, or town. What a repercussion would such a practice have upon our land if the Church of Jesus Christ were to observe the Lord's Day in this way! They did it under law—He still expects it under grace.

2

THE SABBATH

Speak unto the children of Israel, and say unto them,
Concerning the feasts of the Lord, which ye shall
proclaim to be holy convocations, even these are my
feasts. Six days shall work be done: but the seventh day is
the sabbath of rest, and holy convocation; ye shall do no
work therein: it is the sabbath of the Lord in all your
dwellings (Lev. 23:2,3).

BEFORE considering the annual conventions of Israel,
known generally as the feasts of the Lord, time must be
given to evaluate the weekly feast which is so often neg-
lected, and yet it was a feast. It was the first on the list and
its observance was much more frequent.

Lest anyone should read this with a biased mind, saying
that this was Jewish or it was under the law, let it be
understood that, while details sometimes change, principles never alter. The principle is that God demanded one
day in seven, nature demands periodical rest, animals re-
quire rest other than nightly sleep, and even machinery
functions better and wears longer when it has periodical
rest. The fact that the Jews kept the seventh day and we the
first is detail. Under law God demanded it, under grace He
desires it. If we love certain people we seek to fulfill their
desires and submit to their wishes because we know that,
by so doing, we please them. Therefore, if God sought
certain things under law, then it is so much more under
grace.

"The sabbath was made for man, and not man for the sabbath: therefore the Son of man is Lord also of the sabbath" (Mark 2:27,28). The sabbath day was not only given by God to man as a day of rest, but God expects man to give the same day back to Him in worship. How few there are who want to give this day to the Lord! Man is prepared to give God anything but time, and yet our times are in His hand. Man will give money, he will make a subscription to anything mentioned to him, he will give his approval to any kind of project the church would suggest—but not time. He considers Sunday to be his, for his recreation, his pleasure, his family, as though it were the business world that gave him the day. Man has completely failed to recognize that it is the Lord's Day, and that He gave it to man; or better, set it apart for man, that in it he might rest from all his labors (which also means that he sees to it that other men also rest from their labors), so that all of us might have time to relax, to think on spiritual things, to read spiritual matter, and to worship God. Let us examine it this way:

(1) *It was given for man's good.* The body needs periodical rest. Man cannot continue seven days a week. Why are hospitals full? Why is it that there are no vacancies in mental institutions? Why is it that the public enemies of health are heart failure and ulcers? Overwork. Man would blame industry or the commercial world for pressure and overworking. We know this is not true. There may be pressure for five days, then man has a sixth day in which he may relax and enjoy his pleasure, and a seventh day to rest and worship God. If he did this he would accomplish much more with less strain. To question this procedure is foolish.

God rested on the seventh day from all His work.

Nature rests—fruit trees do not bear fruit every year.

Ground needs to be rested—so the farmer leaves his

land fallow, or entirely changes his crop.

Machinery will operate better if it is allowed to rest.

(2) *It was given for worship.* While the day was given for rest, it was not given for indolence. While the body rests, the mind is kept active with the things of the Spirit. Man could worship any day; in fact he should worship every day. However, collective worship is obviously best when we can blend our voices in praise and listen to the exposition of the Word. Therefore it is necessary to have a set time. Unless there is a designated period there would be the risk that worship would soon cease to be.

If it could be realized what life would be like should this day of worship be taken away, most of us would value it more than we do.

(3) *It was given by God.* If it be God's day then it is a holy day, not a holiday, a day to be spent for spiritual profit, not for selfish pleasure; a day to be spent in worship, not a day at work. "Six days shall work be done: but the seventh day is the sabbath of rest, an holy convocation; ye shall do no work therein: it is the sabbath of the Lord in all your dwellings" (Lev. 23:3).

In some of the feasts no servile work was to be done, which means the employment of servants. In other feasts, including the sabbath, "Ye shall do no work." This is all-embracive. No man should work, servant nor master, maid nor mistress. It was a day of rest, absolute and complete, not only in the home but everywhere, for the expression "in all your dwellings" infers "in all parts of the land and out of it," wherever the Jew might be living.

What a wonderful experience it would be if we could see *everything* at a standstill on a Sunday, no work being done, no one employed, all noise being silenced, people walking to church quietly and completely relaxed. That in itself, apart from the spiritual import, would be of immense value to mankind and to the nation, because we would be more relaxed through the week, pressures would yield, and we would be considerably healthier. The reaction would be seen in hospitals, in mental institutions, everywhere.

Some may say that this is impossible. There is nothing that is impossible. If a nation can change the whole of its policies in a time of war, if we can adjust to rations in war, if we can put satellites into space and also rendezvous in space, then this could be done if we had the desire. Some will assert that this was for the Jewish people, and does not apply in the present dispensation. Then it must be understood that the Sabbath Day was not given by Moses nor yet given to Moses. It existed long before the nation of Israel. The day is as old as man. God created man on the sixth day: "And on the seventh day God ended his work which he had made; and he rested on the seventh day from all his work which had had made. And God blessed the seventh day, and sanctified it." This means that it was set apart from the beginning of time. Later, this seventh day was incorporated into the law as the people were reminded to keep it holy.

The fourth commandment is the only one not repeated in the New Testament. Under the old order rest came at the end, but under the new order we commence with rest, because the Lord met all the demands of the law and we rest in an already finished work. Therefore, under grace, the first day of the week became the day set apart for rest and worship. Whether it be the seventh day for the Jew or the first day for the Christian, the principle remains exactly the same. One day in seven should be given to God. If we fail to make this day a day set apart to God and to the things that belong to the Spirit, then we have failed God and failed ourselves.

Exodus 12.

3

THE FEAST OF THE PASSOVER

And the Lord spake unto Moses and Aaron in the land of Egypt, saying, This month shall be unto you the beginning of months: it shall be the first month of the year to you. Speak ye unto all the congregation of Israel, saying, In the tenth day of this month they shall take to them every man a lamb, according to the house of their fathers, a lamb for an house: and if the household be too little for the lamb, let him and his neighbour next unto his house take it according to the number of the souls; every man according to his eating shall make your count for the lamb. Your lamb shall be without blemish, a male of the first year: ye shall take it out from the sheep, or from the goats: and ye shall keep it up until the fourteenth day of the same month: and the whole assembly of the congregation of Israel shall kill it in the evening. And they shall take of the blood, and strike it on the two side posts and on the upper door post of the houses, wherein they shall eat it. And they shall eat the flesh in that night, roast with fire, and unleavened bread; and with bitter herbs they shall eat it. Eat not of it raw, nor sodden at all with water, but roast with fire; his head with his legs, and with the purtenance thereof. And ye shall let nothing of it remain until the morning; and that which remaineth of it until the morning ye shall burn with fire. And thus shall ye eat it; with your loins girded, your shoes on your feet, and your staff in your hand; and ye shall eat it in haste: it is the Lord's passover. For I will

pass through the land of Egypt this night, and will smite
all the firstborn in the land of Egypt, both man and
beast; and against all the gods of Egypt I will execute
judgment: I am the Lord. And the blood shall be to you
for a token upon the houses where ye are: and when I
see the blood, I will pass over you, and the plague shall
not be upon you to destroy you, when I smite the land of
Egypt. And this day shall be unto you for a memorial;
and ye shall keep it a feast to the Lord throughout your
generations; ye shall keep it a feast by an ordinance for
ever. Seven days shall ye eat unleavened bread; even the
first day ye shall put away leaven out of your houses: for
whosoever eateth leavened bread from the first day
until the seventh day, that soul shall be cut off from
Israel. And in the first day there shall be an holy convocation, and in the seventh day there shall be an holy
convocation to you; no manner of work shall be done in
them, save that which every man must eat, that only may
be done of you. And ye shall observe the feast of unleavened bread; for in this self-same day have I brought
your armies out of the land of Egypt: therefore shall ye
observe this day in your generations by an ordinance for
ever. In the first month, on the fourteenth day of the
month at even, ye shall eat unleavened bread, until the
one and twentieth day of the month at even. Seven days
shall there be no leaven found in your houses: for
whosoever eateth that which is leavened, even that soul
shall be cut off from the congregation of Israel, whether
he be a stranger, or born in the land. Ye shall eat nothing
leavened; in all your habitations shall ye eat unleavened
bread. Then Moses called for all the elders of Israel, and
said unto them, Draw out and take you a lamb according
to your families, and kill the passover. And ye shall take
a bunch of hyssop, and dip it in the blood that is in the
bason, and strike the lintel and the two side posts with
the blood that is in the bason; and none of you shall go
out at the door of his house until the morning. For the
Lord will pass through to smite the Egyptians; and when

he seeth the blood upon the lintel, and on the two side posts, the Lord will pass over the door, and will not suffer the destroyer to come in unto your houses to smite you. And ye shall observe this thing for an ordinance to thee and to thy sons for ever. And it shall come to pass, when ye be come to the land which the Lord will give you, according as He hath promised, that ye shall keep this service. And it shall come to pass, when your children shall say unto you, What mean ye by this service? that ye shall say, It is the sacrifice of the Lord's passover, who passed over the houses of the children of Israel in Egypt, when He smote the Egyptians, and delivered our houses. And the people bowed the head and worshipped. And the children of Israel went away, and did as the Lord had commanded Moses and Aaron, so did they. And it came to pass that at midnight the Lord smote all the firstborn in the land of Egypt, from the firstborn of Pharaoh that sat on his throne unto the firstborn of the captive that was in the dungeon; and all the firstborn of cattle. And Pharaoh rose up in the night, he, and all his servants, and all the Egyptians; and there was a great cry in Egypt; for there was not a house where there was not one dead (Exod. 12:1–30).

THIS account is well known as it has been retold so many times; therefore, the salient points of the story will suffice.

Israel had been in Egypt a long time (in fact, 430 years—Exod. 12:40), and many changes had taken place. Their entrance into the land had everything in their favor, with all the blessings of Pharaoh resting upon them. Their exit was very different; indeed, nothing was in their favor. Instead of enjoying the freedom of the land, they had become slaves; instead of having the best, they were enduring the worst the taskmasters could lay on them; instead of the blessings of Pharaoh, it was the cursings of another Pharaoh "who knew not Joseph," a ruler who was fearful of the power that might be manifested by an alien people within his domain; and yet, while all this was true, their sufferings, like most of ours, were self-imposed, brought upon them by their own self-will and rebellion. The first Pharaoh had been favorable to them because they were in favor with God. The last Pharaoh was opposing them because they, as a people, were opposing God and, therefore, God had turned His back upon them.

Now God had heard their cry, and was coming down to deliver them. Not only was He about to bring deliverance to His own people, but He was also in the process of punishing the nation that had found delight in being cruel to the children of Israel. Already God had inflicted nine plagues upon the Egyptians, every one of them proving how helpless were the gods of Egypt, for the Israelites had been immune to every plague. Egypt's gods had not checked one of the plagues nor alleviated the sufferings of their worshipers. The tenth and final plague was about to be administered. It was the death of the firstborn of every Egyptian family, including the royal household. Not only was this to be a great tragedy in the social life of all Egypt, but it was to be the greatest blow to their religious system, for the Egyptians never accepted death. They abominated the thought of it, and as a result they worshiped everything that symbolized life. They believed in the transmigration of spirits, and so made preparation for the journey of that spirit into its next realm.

This event was going to be so sudden and so disastrous that the Lord began to prepare His people for their emancipation before the blow fell upon the nation, and to enable His people to make a complete exodus before Pharaoh could again change his mind. The plan was made by God. The instructions were clear and simple. The scheme might not appear logical in the thinking of man, but all that was required was obedience.

The event was going to be so stupendous in the lives of

these oppressed people and in the future of their nation that God changed the calendar. It happened in the fourth month of the year, but God said: "This month shall be unto you the beginning of months: it shall be the first month of the year to you" (Exod. 12:2). The rest of the story will be considered under the title

The Feast. Much of it became an annual event. On the tenth day of the month a lamb had to be taken for each family. It was to be kept for four days to prove it was without blemish. On the fourteenth day it was slain and the blood was sprinkled upon the two door posts and the upper lintel, for protection from the angel of death came only by *applied* blood. Blood in a bowl in the house, or blood shed, was not sufficient. It had to be applied where it could be seen, for, said the Lord: ". . . when I see the blood, I will pass over you, and the plague shall not be upon you to destroy you, when I smite the land of Egypt" (Exod. 12:13). Salvation is not our project—it is His provision.

Inside the house, protected by that blood, the people prepared to feast upon the lamb that had been slain. The feast also included bitter herbs and unleavened bread. Instead of taking the meal leisurely, they were required to have their loins girded as for a journey, their shoes on their feet, their staves in their hands, ready to make a speedy exit, for the day of their emancipation had come. God was meting out vengeance upon their enemies, and upon Pharaoh who had so stubbornly refused to let them go. He was now prepared to drive them out. When God's time had fully come bondage was suddenly changed into glorious liberty. This was the beginning of a new life. Therefore they had to leave the old conditions before they became entangled again.

This feast, as considered so far, was a historical event. It took place once only. However, certain events were established to be observed annually as memorials lest the people should forget the goodness of God. Thus we read: "These are the feasts of the Lord, even holy convocations, which ye shall proclaim in their seasons. In the fourteenth day of the first month at even is the Lord's passover" (Lev. 23:4,5).

Antitype. This Feast is not only kept as a commemorative rite to remind Israel of a past deliverance, but it is also an occasion to remind these people of a greater deliverance yet to come.

When Jesus began His public ministry ". . . John seeth Jesus coming unto him, and saith, Behold the Lamb of God, which taketh away the sin of the world" (John 1:29). For years the Jewish nation had offered a lamb from the first Passover night until the days of the New Testament. That lamb had reminded them of God's past deliverance. Now John was pointing out to these same people that before them stood *the* Lamb of God, the One whom they had long anticipated. God was now turning their shadows into substance, their anticipations into realization, the type into antitype. Here was the Emancipator, the One who was to pardon all sin.

The Passover lamb of the commemorative rite had to be kept four days before it was slain to establish proof that it was without blemish. *The* Lamb of God, now introduced to the nation, engaged in three and a half years of public ministry where all could behold Him, check His life and ministry, and establish the fact that He was without sin, the perfect Son of God. This evidence was given just before He died:

Judas said: "I have sinned in that I have betrayed the innocent blood" (Matt. 27:4).

Pilate said: "I am innocent of the blood of this just person" (Matt. 27:24).

Pilate's wife said: "Have thou nothing to do with that

just man" (Matt. 27:19).

Pilate said: "I find in Him no fault at all" (John 18:38).

The malefactor said: "This man hath done nothing amiss" (Luke 23:41).

The centurion said: "Truly this man was the Son of God" (Mark 15:39).

These testimonies concerning the sinless One all came from His enemies and from the world. Peter, Stephen, and Paul bore the same record, and so did His Father.

Without blemish though He was, yet He was taken by wicked hands and crucified. Paul referring back to this said: "For even Christ our passover is sacrificed for us" (1 Cor. 5:7). ". . . and without shedding of blood is no remission" (Heb. 9:22).

Spiritual Application—*Salvation.* It must be borne in mind that by nature we are sinners, and that we are in the Egypt of this world which is ruled over by Satan. Under his régime men become slaves and are doomed to eternal destruction.

In this helpless condition that was the lot of man, God sent His Son to become the Lamb of God. As the Lamb He died at Calvary, that through the shedding of His Blood salvation might come to all men. The event is history. It may be called religion, doctrine, theology, or anything else, but it was God's plan and there is no alternative. One of the great essentials in the Passover story was that man had to take the blood of the lamb and apply it to his own house, with the promise: "When I see the blood I will pass over you." This essential remains true today. It is not sufficient to be born in a country called "Christian" because it accepts certain facts of history, or because one finds himself in a Christian community where he has been taught to go to church and to accept in principle the things preached there. There must be a personal acceptance of the blood of Jesus Christ applied to the heart and life, an individual understanding that Christ died for *my* sin, that His Blood accepted can wash away *my* sin, and that in so doing the condemnation of death which is *my* due can be removed.

This act, whereby we accept in simple faith and obedience the efficacy of the blood of Christ shed upon the cross as the cleansing for our sin, is called

Salvation. Man passes from death unto life, from bondage into liberty, from darkness into light. He is leaving an old life for a new one. He is entering into an entirely new experience.

Having walked to God through sacrifice, he now begins his walk with God through separation; in other words, salvation is not an end, it is a beginning. Hence the Lord says: "This month shall be to you the beginning of months."

This life should be one of great excitement as the believer grows from the babe in Christ into the mature life of the disciple. Spiritual life must know the same growth, development of character, and maturity of experience, which takes place in the natural life, but with one tremendous difference. In the physical body a certain point of development is reached, and then, suddenly, it is realized that we have gone over the hill, and now there is ever the reminder of decline, mental alertness gives way, the memory fails, the energy weakens, and we are reminded that, whatever has been accomplished in the realm of success, whatever has been acquired in material possessions, however great the host of friends we have made, one day we shall lose everything. The finality of the physical realm is death, and as surely as we brought nothing into the world, so surely we will take nothing out of it. The soul, which knows no death, leaves this present world to inhabit another realm.

The thrill and excitement of this new life, which is

inherited at salvation, is one of continuous development and knows no end. The physical body declines, but the spiritual soul matures. Earthly success terminates, but spiritual success has rewards awaiting in the life to come. While material possessions are left behind, spiritual possessions are treasures laid up in heaven where neither moth nor rust corrupt and where thieves do not break through nor steal. We may bid adieu to our friends on earth, but the Christian is reunited with them in heaven. We anticipate the fellowship of heaven.

Our journey is toward a promised inheritance and an eternal rest. Having begun this walk on earth, let us take the next step.

4

THE FEAST OF UNLEAVENED BREAD

Seven days shall ye eat unleavened bread; even the first day ye shall put away leaven out of your houses: for whosoever eateth leavened bread from the first day until the seventh day, that soul shall be cut off from Israel. And in the first day there shall be an holy convocation, and in the seventh day there shall be an holy convocation to you; no manner of work shall be done in them, save that which every man must eat, that only may be done of you. And ye shall observe the feast of unleavened bread; for in this selfsame day have I brought your armies out of the land of Egypt: therefore shall ye observe this day in your generations by an ordinance for ever. In the first month, on the fourteenth day of the month at even, ye shall eat unleavened bread, until the one and twentieth day of the month at even. Seven days shall there be no leaven found in your houses: for whosoever eateth that which is leavened, even that soul shall be cut off from the congregation of Israel, whether he be a stranger, or born in the land. Ye shall eat nothing leavened; in all your habitations shall ye eat unleavened bread (Exod. 12:15–20).

And Moses said unto the people, Remember this day, in which ye came out from Egypt, out of the house of bondage; for by strength of hand the Lord brought you out from this place: there shall no leavened bread be eaten. This day came ye out in the month Abib. And it shall be when the Lord shall bring thee into the land of the Canaanites, and the Hittites, and the Amorites, and the Hivites, and the Jebusites, which he sware unto thy fathers to give thee, a land flowing with milk and honey, that thou shalt keep this service in this month. Seven days thou shalt eat unleavened bread, and in the seventh day shall be a feast to the Lord. Unleavened bread shall be eaten seven days; and there shall no leavened bread be seen with thee, neither shall there be leaven seen with thee in all thy quarters. And thou shalt shew thy son in that day, saying, This is done because of that which the Lord did unto me when I came forth out of Egypt. And it shall be for a sign unto thee upon thine hand, and for a memorial between thine eyes, that the Lord's law may be in thy mouth: for with a strong hand hath the Lord brought thee out of Egypt. Thou shalt therefore keep this ordinance in his season from year to year (Exod. 13:3–10).

THE Feast of unleavened bread was included in the Passover feast, which accounts for the overlap of dates. Both feasts commenced on the fourteenth day of the first month. The one was a single day celebration, the other was observed for seven days. The number seven being symbolic of completeness means that whatever was inferred by the feast involved the complete life. There are many scattered scriptures which, when brought together, make a complete picture.

The Feast. "In the first month, on the fourteenth day of the month at even, ye shall eat unleavened bread, until the one and twentieth day of the month at even. Seven days shall there be no leaven found in your houses: for whosoever eateth that which is leavened, even that soul shall be cut off from the congregation of Israel, whether he be a stranger, or born in the land. Ye shall eat nothing leavened; in all your habitations shall ye eat unleavened bread" (Exod. 12:18–20).

Although the feast of unleavened bread as such commenced on the fifteenth day, "on the fifteenth day of the same month is the feast of unleavened bread unto the Lord . . ." (Lev. 23:6), yet unleavened bread was not to be eaten at the Passover which was on the fourteenth day. Therefore, the day before was called "the day of preparation." "Now the next day, that followed the day of preparation. . ." (Matt. 27:62). "And it was the preparation of the passover . . ." (John 19:14).

This day involved a great time of spring-cleaning. No leaven was allowed within their dwellings. It meant more than not eating leaven. It was a matter of complete separation. This, therefore, meant a great deal of activity for the woman. Everything in the house had to be cleansed thoroughly. The ceilings and walls were washed, floors and cupboards were scrubbed, corners were scoured, and every piece of furniture cleaned. All the cooking utensils were boiled in water and put away, while special utensils and ovens were brought into use, things that had never been contaminated by leaven in the course of the year. So thoroughly was this work done that the woman would have a pointed implement with which she would scrape through every crack or joint, impression or corner, any spot where, during the year, a crumb of bread containing leaven might have settled. The law was that no leaven should remain anywhere within their dwellings. They carried out the law strictly to the letter.

When the cleansing was complete, a member of the household would take pieces of leavened break and tuck each piece in hiding places, somewhere around the house—a piece under a cushion, or on a ledge, or behind a vessel. At the day's close, when the man of the house had returned from the fields and had partaken of his evening meal, and after the sun had set, there would take place in each home the ceremony known as the search for leaven.

Taking a lighted candle, a feather brush, and a wooden spoon, the father would search for the pieces of leavened bread which had previously been hidden. The children, who had earlier taken note of where the bread had been placed, would help father by telling him that he was getting hot and hotter, or cold and colder, as he advanced toward or retreated from the various pieces (a game with which many of us are acquainted). As he gathered each piece he would recite a prayer: "Blessed art Thou, O Lord our God, King of the Universe, who hast sanctified us with Thy commandments and commanded us to remove the leaven."

He then wrapped the pieces in a cloth and said: "All kinds of leaven that are in my possession which I have not observed nor removed, shall be null and counted as the dust of the earth." Next morning, with similar prayers, he burned the pieces.

Having done all that was within their power to remove the leaven, they trusted God to annul or destroy anything they had accidentally missed. They were now ready for the observance of the feast.

Only unleavened bread was to be eaten. This was made of white flour, ground in special mills and superintended by a wise man of the law. The dough was made of flour and water only. No salt must be added. It was then rolled into flat cakes, pierced and pricked all over, and baked in a specially prepared oven, very hot. On this bread the children of Israel lived for eight days.

It is recorded in the book of Exodus how all of these commands and observances were passed down from generation to generation. "And thou shalt shew thy son in that day, saying, This is done because of that which the Lord did unto me when I came forth out of Egypt" (Exod. 13:8).

The whole of this feast was to teach the people that they

were to be disassociated from the old life. They were to keep themselves from the carnalities of the world around them. They were a holy people separated to the Lord their God. Leaven was a type of that world.

Lest they should forget this requirement of God, He established this feast to be an annual event and hence a constant reminder.

It is generally believed that the children of Israel ate unleavened bread at the Passover Feast in Egypt. They did not. Leaven belonged to Egypt and the world. It was a type of sin and belonged to the old life. The unleavened bread belonged to the new life. The evidence that they did not eat this bread in Egypt is seen in the haste with which they left the land. Through the urgency of the Egyptians, the people were driven out before they had a chance to cook their bread. "And the people took their dough before it was leavened, their kneading-troughs being bound up in their clothes upon their shoulders ... And the children of Israel journeyed from Rameses to Succoth" (Exod. 12:34,37).

It has been said that unleavened bread belonged to the new life. The bread they carried out of Egypt they ate at Succoth in the wilderness. "And the children of Israel journeyed from Rameses to Succoth, about six hundred thousand on foot that were men, beside children. And a mixed multitude went up also with them; and flocks, and herds, even very much cattle. And they baked *unleavened cakes of the dough which they brought forth out of Egypt,* for it was not leavened; because they were thrust out of Egypt and could not tarry, neither had they prepared for themselves any victual" (Exod. 12:37-39).

Antitype. As the Jew in the Old Testament was very conscientious about being rid of all leaven for the particular period, so the same truth is propounded in the New Testament concerning this, the church age, and must become the responsibility of every believer in Christ.

Paul, writing to the saints in the Corinthian church, left us without any shadow of a doubt: "Purge out therefore the old leaven, that ye may be a new lump, as ye are unleavened. For even Christ our Passover is sacrificed for us: therefore let us keep the feast, not with old leaven, neither with the leaven of malice and wickedness; but with the unleavened bread of sincerity and truth (1 Cor. 5:7, 8).

Leaven is that which promotes fermentation and corruption. A little of it will bring a whole batch of dough into an upheaval. It quickly permeates the whole. As a result it is used in Scripture as a type of sin. Sin had crept into the Corinthian church. Paul required that this leaven should be removed from that church because God demanded holiness.

When Paul wrote to them he was not writing to sinners but to the saints who had been responsible for allowing this intrusion. Sin is like leaven. A little of it goes a long way, and its influence is considerable.

God's concern for Israel was contamination, the influence that the nations around could have upon a separated nation. It was for the same reason the Lord would not allow His people to intermingle through marriage. "Wherefore come out from among them, and be ye separate, saith the Lord, and touch not the unclean thing; and I will receive you, and will be a father unto you, and ye shall be my sons and daughters, saith the Lord Almighty" (2 Cor. 6:17,18).

Spiritual Application—*Separation*. As surely as the feast of unleavened bread immediately followed the Passover and was, in fact, a part of it, so the life of sanctification, the life that is one of separation from the world, the flesh, and the devil, commences with our salvation and should continue for the remainder of life's journey on earth, inasmuch as the period of seven days is the symbol of the complete life. This life is not one that should ever be reached after and never attained. It should be an experience to be enjoyed at all times. In salvation the believer dies to self that he may live for Christ, hence he has a new life which must have new experiences and is lived by His enabling. It is a life totally different from the one that belonged to the world, for it is the outliving of his indwelling.

Many people have the idea that a nation refrained from eating unleavened bread for a week, but let the fact be underscored that no leaven was to be found within their dwelling—it was not to be within the camp.

May we be permitted to use a personal illustration. The author, in one of his earlier pastorates, went to his church each morning for a period of time in order to make a church alteration. He went in by a back door and stayed the whole morning. The church was situated on a main road facing a row of shops. A member of the church, a teenage girl who was not working at the time, discovered the situation. About an hour later each morning she wandered into the church by the same door, and just stood around talking. This she did to pass her time away, having nothing else to do. This happened for three mornings. On the fourth day when she arrived, he took her to the front of the church and, opening the front doors, pointed out to the girl that on the other side of the street was a shoe-repairer sitting in the window, and a butcher and a greengrocer both serving merchandise from open windows. The probability was that these people had witnessed the arrival of the minister and, later, the arrival of the girl. This would suggest that a man and a girl were together in a closed church. Might not the situation put thoughts and ideas into the minds of these people? Was it not possible that, although the girl came in innocently to have a chat, rumors might be put into circulation that could be damaging to the church? The girl was told to go home and never to come into the church again when the pastor was there alone. This decision was made in order to "abstain from all *appearance* of evil" (1 Thess. 5:22).

It is not enough that we do not commit sin, but we must walk so circumspectly that we do not give the world a single advantage whereby it may accuse us. Are we living this life, or are we so mixed up with the world, with worldly ambitions, and participating in the pleasures, fashions, and customs of the world, that it becomes difficult to distinguish the one from the other?

Must we not also confess that a great deal of the world and its carnalities have crept into the church? In our compromise to win the world, we have lost the world and our own testimony.

This is God's claim on a regenerate life. Have we made this second step? Is our all upon the altar? Is He our satisfying portion? Are we living the life that is dead to self and alive to Christ? If so, we are ready for the next step in this "Walk with God through separation."

5

THE FEAST OF FIRSTFRUITS

And the Lord spake unto Moses, saying, Speak unto the children of Israel, and say unto them, When ye be come into the land which I give unto you, and shall reap the harvest thereof, then ye shall bring a sheaf of the firstfruits of your harvest unto the priest: and he shall wave the sheaf before the Lord, to be accepted for you: on the morrow after the sabbath the priest shall wave it. And ye shall offer that day when ye wave the sheaf an he lamb without blemish of the first year for a burnt offering unto the Lord. And the meat offering thereof shall be two tenth deals of fine flour mingled with oil, an offering made by fire unto the Lord for a sweet savour: and the drink offering thereof shall be of wine, the fourth part of an hin. And ye shall eat neither bread, nor parched corn, nor green ears, until the selfsame day that ye have brought an offering unto your God: it shall be a statute for ever throughout your generations in all your dwellings (Lev. 23:9–14).

THIS feast was closely associated with the two that have gone before, inasmuch as all were under the major subject of Passover, and were held consecutively on the fourteenth, fifteenth, and sixteenth days of the first month. Although the Passover was established on the night they left Egypt, it was not observed as a commemorative feast throughout the forty years they were wandering in the wilderness. This could not be because they had no lambs, or because the people were being sustained by the manna which God provided from day to day. After keeping the Passover on the night of their deliverance, they never observed it again until they entered the Promised Land. "And the children of Israel encamped in Gilgal, and kept the Passover on the fourteenth day of the month at even in the plains of Jericho" (Joshua 5.10).

Likewise, this feast of firstfruits was not observed until the nation had entered the Promised Land. Until this time they had eaten only manna. In the desert a roaming people had no fields to sow nor harvests to reap. "Speak unto the children of Israel, and say unto them, *When ye come into the land* which I give unto you, and shall reap the harvest thereof, then ye shall bring a sheaf of the firstfruits of your harvest unto the priest" (Lev. 23:10). This would be barley because it was the first grain to ripen. After the barley would come the harvesting of the fruit, the olives, the vintage, and finally the wheat.

The Feast. The account of the feast, so far as the ceremony in the house of God was concerned, is recorded in Leviticus 23. However, it is necessary to turn to the pages of history and to the customs of these people in order to gain information as to the preliminaries to the feast.

At the time of seed sowing, members of the Sanhedrin would have marked off certain barley by going out to three of the fields within the vicinity of the city and laying in each field a hoop, thereby ringing off that seed. These were left until the seed germinated, sprang up, and matured. By the time the harvest season arrived, the hoops would be hidden under the ripened grain.

It must be borne in mind that this feast was kept on the sixteenth day, and that at that time the day began at six o'clock in the evening (hence the repeated statement in

Genesis 1: "And the evening and the morning were a day.") Toward the close of the fifteenth day, just before the going down of the sun, three men, each carrying a sickle and a basket, walked out through the city gate. Separating, each one would move toward one of the three buried hoops, and there stand. These men would be accompanied by representatives of the people, both religious and secular—in other words, elders and priests— who would wait outside the city gate. Quietly they would watch the sun set, denoting the end of that day. As it slipped over the horizon the three men would address the priest with the following questions:

Has the sun gone down?

On this fifteenth day?

Into this basket? (Each man would hold the basket above his head).

With this sickle? (Holding it high for all to see).

Shall I reap?

To each question the priest would answer in the affirmative. With the last "yes," the three men simultaneously would thrust their sickles into the barley within the hoops, and the sheaves would be placed in the baskets. Then these men, with the priests and elders, would march processionally up to the temple with much rejoicing, where the bundles would be put together into one great sheaf and handed to the priest. He, in turn, took the sheaf and waved it before the Lord as a wave offering: ". . . When ye be come into the land which I give unto you, and shall reap the harvest thereof, then ye shall bring a sheaf of the first-fruits of your harvest unto the priest: and he shall wave the sheaf before the Lord, to be accepted for you: on the morrow after the sabbath the priest shall wave it" (Lev. 23:10,11). This wave sheaf was accompanied by burnt and meal offerings.

Until the wave sheaf was offered ". . . ye shall eat

neither bread, nor parched corn, nor green ears, until the selfsame day that ye have brought an offering unto your God . . ." (Lev. 23:14). This meant that no man was permitted to partake of any part of the new season's harvest until the firstfruits had been presented.

The act of waving the sheaf from one side to the other before the Lord held the suggestion that the sheaf, which was a memorial, was waved sideways to indicate that it represented the whole harvest yet in the field, from one side of the land to the other side of the land.

In brief, men gave thanks to God for the harvest while it still stood in the fields. God always claimed firstfruits of everything. He still does.

Antitype. What a wonderful picture of our Lord Jesus Christ who, having become the Paschal Lamb shedding His blood upon the cross, is afterwards seen in the fullness of His resurrection power. Said Paul: "But now is Christ risen from the dead, and become the *firstfruits* of them that slept" (1 Cor. 15:20). He was the corn of wheat which fell into the ground and died, that it might spring up again and have much fruit. The feast of firstfruits was the third day from Passover. Christ rose as the firstfruits of resurrection on the third day from His death.

As the sheaf was a memorial or a representation of the whole harvest in the field, so Christ, when He arose from the dead, said to Mary: ". . . Touch me not; for I am not yet ascended (I am ascending) to my Father: but go to my brethren, and say unto them, I ascend unto my Father, and your Father; and to my God, and your God" (John 20:17).

The Lord is now in the presence of His Father as the representative of the whole Church of Jesus Christ still in the field. He has promised: ". . . because I live, ye shall live also." He will remain the firstfruits and our representative until the day of His coming again, when the whole harvest of the Church, including those who are in the graves and we who are alive and remain, shall be gathered in for the great "Harvest Home."

When the sheaves were cut from the fields and carried to the city, small vacant spots were left behind. When the Lord rose from the dead, He left behind Him a small vacant spot, which still remains as a reminder of His resurrection—it is an empty tomb.

During the time the grain was growing in the field, it enjoyed the warmth of the sun and withstood the winds, storms, and all the adverse weather elements. Thus it is with the child of God. So long as he is in this world he will know something of the adverse wind, the storm, and drought, that toss him about at times and wilt his faith at other times, but he can also bask in the warmth of God's love and find the reinvigoration that comes in the rays of His mercy and in the dew of His grace. It takes all of these experiences, the adverse and the acceptable, to develop our fruitfulness so that we will not be ashamed at His coming. Remember that the Sheaf of Firstfruits, who has gone before, knew all these same experiences.

Spiritual Application—*Consecration.* This is the third step in the Christian walk—the first, salvation; the second, separation; the third, consecration. Separation, as seen in the unleavened bread, far-reaching as it was, proved to be insufficient of itself. At least God thought so, for He required more. Likewise, separation in the Christian life is not the beginning and end of God's requirements—He asks for consecration.

A question which might come immediately to mind would be—What is the difference? In the first, it is separation *from;* in the second, separation *to.* If one only separates from the world, or from anything else, and seeks to stand alone, he could very readily become an isolationist. This is not practicable because there is too much involved in life. The Lord illustrated this point with a parable told in Luke 11:17–26. The Lord was casting out devils. He was separating a man from the power of an old life, and there were those who questioned His authority. In His reply to His critics He said that a kingdom divided against itself would fall, and a house divided against itself would fall. Division is a weakening thing in itself, and the reason is "When the unclean spirit is gone out of a man, he walketh through dry places, seeking rest; and finding none, he saith, I will return unto my house whence I came out. And when he cometh, he findeth it swept and garnished. Then goeth he, and taketh to him seven other spirits more wicked than himself; and they enter in, and dwell there: and the last state of that man is worse than the first." If a person leaves one thing he must be attached to something else. He cannot be independent. To think that salvation means only separation from the world is a tragedy, because although we may not be of the world, we are in it and we are surrounded; in fact, we are pressured by its temptations, its pleasures, its moral issues in business, as well as in its social and political life. It is impossible for any individual to resist this mass force. Therefore, immediately we separate *from* the old life, we must separate ourselves *unto* the Lord Jesus Christ, the only source of power. This is what is understood by consecration.

It will be easy to appreciate the thought sought to be conveyed by seeing it in operation in everyday life.

A piece of land is consecrated when it is separated *to* burial—A cemetery.

A building is consecrated when it is separated *to* the worship of God—A church.

A man is consecrated when he is separated *to* the work of the ministry—A minister.

We consecrate ourselves when we separate our lives and will *to* the purposes of God.

It must be emphasized that this feast was held on the

sixteenth day, and the third step of the Passover, or salvation. The believer, therefore, gives the firstfruits of his life, the best part of it, the early years if converted early—yea, himself—and yields them without reserve to the Lord remembering ". . . ye are not your own. For ye are bought with a price: therefore glorify God in your body, and in your spirit, which are God's" (1 Cor. 6:19,20).

As no person was allowed to move a sickle in the field until the firstfruits were presented, so we take nothing to ourselves until we have presented our all to Him.

> My spirit, soul, and body,
> Jesus, I give to Thee,
> A consecrated off'ring,
> Thine evermore to be.
> My all is on the altar,
> Lord, I am all Thine own;
> Oh, may my faith ne'er falter,
> Lord, keep me Thine alone.

When we have yielded our all, then He will give us back our lives, endued, equipped, blessed.

> Take my life, and let it be
> Consecrated, Lord, to Thee.

6

THE FEAST OF PENTECOST

And ye shall count unto you from the morrow after the sabbath, from the day that ye brought the sheaf of the wave offering; seven sabbaths shall be complete: even unto the morrow after the seventh sabbath shall ye number fifty days; and ye shall offer a new meat offering unto the Lord. Ye shall bring out of your habitations two wave loaves of two tenth deals: they shall be of fine flour; they shall be baken with leaven; they are the firstfruits unto the Lord. And ye shall offer with the bread seven lambs without blemish of the first year, and one young bullock, and two rams: they shall be for a burnt offering unto the Lord, with their meat offering, and their drink offerings, even an offering made by fire, of sweet savour unto the Lord. Then ye shall sacrifice one kid of the goats for a sin offering, and two lambs of the first year for a sacrifice of peace offerings. And the priest shall wave them with the bread of the firstfruits for a wave offering before the Lord, with the two lambs: they shall be holy to the Lord for the priest. And ye shall proclaim on the selfsame day, that it may be an holy convocation unto you: ye shall do no servile work therein: it shall be a statute for ever in all your dwellings throughout your generations. And when ye reap the harvest of your land, thou shalt not make clean riddance of the corners of thy field when thou reapest, neither shalt thou gather any gleaning of thy harvest: thou shalt leave them unto the poor, and to the stranger: I am the

Lord your God (Lev. 23:15–22).

And when the day of Pentecost was fully come, they were all with one accord in one place. And suddenly there came a sound from heaven as of a rushing mighty wind, and it filled all the house where they were sitting. And there appeared unto them cloven tongues like as of fire, and it sat upon each of them. And they were all filled with the Holy Ghost, and began to speak with other tongues, as the Spirit gave them utterance. And there were dwelling at Jerusalem Jews, devout men, out of every nation under heaven. Now when this was noised abroad, the multitude came together, and were confounded, because that every man heard them speak in his own language. And they were all amazed and marvelled, saying one to another, Behold, are not all these which speak Galilaeans? And how hear we every man in our own tongue, wherein we were born? Parthians, and Medes, and Elamites, and the dwellers in Mesopotamia, and in Judaea, and Cappadocia, in Pontus, and Asia, Phrygia, and Pamphylia, in Egypt, and in the parts of Libya about Cyrene, and strangers of Rome, Jews and proselytes, Cretes and Arabians, we do hear them speak in our tongues the wonderful works of God. And they were all amazed, and were in doubt, saying one to another, What meaneth this? Others mocking said, These men are full of new wine. But Peter, standing up with the eleven, lifted up his voice, and said unto them, Ye men of Judaea, and all ye that dwell at Jerusalem, be this known unto you, and hearken to my words: for these are not drunken, as ye suppose, seeing it is but the third hour of the day, but this is that which was spoken by the prophet Joel; And it shall come to pass in the last days, saith God, I will pour out of my Spirit upon all flesh: and your sons and your daughters shall prophesy, and your young men shall see visions, and your old men shall dream dreams: and on my servants and on my handmaidens I will pour out in those days of my Spirit; and they shall prophesy: and I will shew wonders in heaven above, and signs in the earth beneath; blood, and fire, and vapour of smoke: the sun shall be turned into darkness, and the moon into blood, before that great and notable day of the Lord come: and it shall come to pass, that whosoever shall call on the name of the Lord shall be saved. . . . Now when they heard this, they were pricked in their heart, and said unto Peter and to the rest of the apostles, Men and brethren, what shall we do? Then Peter said unto them, Repent, and be baptized every one of you in the name of Jesus Christ for the remission of sins, and ye shall receive the gift of the Holy Ghost. For the promise is unto you, and to your children, and to all that are afar off, even as many as the Lord our God shall call. And with many other words did he testify and exhort, saying, Save yourselves from this untoward generation. Then they that gladly received his word were baptized: and the same day there were added unto them about three thousand souls (Acts 2:1–41).

FOLLOWING the feast of firstfruits there were no other feasts for seven weeks, even though the period is sometimes called the "feast of weeks." The children of Israel having presented their firstfruits to God, and He having received them, the harvesting began. This was a busy season for the people. It took the whole seven weeks for the ingathering. It has already been mentioned that it began with the barley harvest, which ripened in April. By the time the barley was in, the fruit was ready, after which the olives were gathered. Then the vineyards became hives of activity with the vintage, and the season concluded with the ingathering of the wheat.

As there was a feast to acknowledge the firstfruits, so there was one to commemorate harvest home. It was called Pentecost, because *pente* in Greek is "fifty," and this took place fifty days after the presentation of the wave sheaf.

Owing to the time element, this feast required a special journey to Jerusalem for all the men of the land. It was a time of great rejoicing for the harvest was now gathered.

The Feast.   The Lord said "And ye shall count unto you from the morrow after the sabbath, from the day that ye brought the sheaf of the wave offering; seven sabbaths shall be complete [that is, seven weeks, or $7 \times 7 = 49$ days]: Even unto the morrow after the seventh sabbath [+ 1 day] shall ye number fifty days; and ye shall offer a new meat offering unto the Lord" (Lev. 23:15,16).

The new meal offering had a number of distinguishing features.

Firstfruits	Pentecost
Barley.	Wheat.
Sheaf of grain.	Two loaves of bread.
No leaven.	Leavened bread
First of the harvest.	Completion of harvest.
Wave Offering.	Wave Offering.

The barley was the food of the poorer people, as the lad with five barley loaves and two small fishes; the wheat, which came later, was more nutritious and was used by the better class.

While it has been observed that Christ was the Firstfruits of the great harvest, that His humiliation was the prelude to a great exultation, it must also be seen that the handful of believers who were present at Christ's resurrection was but the small foretaste of the great multitude which will be ingathered at Christ's second advent. In all the work of the Lord, His gifts to His Church, and the spiritual blessings, are an ever-increasing, enriching experience.

The difference between a sheaf of grain and a loaf of bread is that the first is made of separate grains, and the second is the same grains consolidated into one loaf. Leaven is in this bread because, although the Lord has willed it otherwise, yet sin is found within the church. It was because of the presence of sin that the sin offering, the burnt offering, and the peace offering were included.

One of the unexpected turns in the account is that the subject is firstfruits, that which was offered before man could begin to harvest, yet the matter of gleanings is included, which belonged to the end of harvest. "And when ye reap the harvest of your land, thou shalt not make clean riddance of the corners of thy field when thou reapest, neither shalt thou gather any gleaning of thy harvest: thou shalt leave them unto the poor, and to the stranger: I am the Lord your God" (Lev. 23:22).

This law, it must be appreciated, was given to the Jews and it concerned their behavior. It was also given to teach them that the blessings of the Lord did not belong to them exclusively, but some of them were to be shared with other peoples. Therefore they were to leave the gleanings of the harvest. These other peoples, the poor and the stranger, could refer to the gentile nations around them, when considered in the realm of spiritual application.

Today things are in the reverse. The Christian church is enjoying the blessings of the Lord and harvesting the fruits of His saving grace. In so doing it must be borne in mind that we are responsible for leaving the gleanings and the corners for those who are not of this fold. In fact, we should be allowing some handfuls to fall on purpose.

Antitype. In the feast of firstfruits Jesus was to be recognized as the One who, having risen from the dead, became the Firstfruits of resurrection. When He said to Mary: "Touch me not, I am ascending," He was presenting Himself to the Father as the wave sheaf. After His resurrection He was seen for forty days, proving his resurrection in the display of those many infallible proofs. "To whom also he shewed himself alive after his passion by many infallible proofs, being seen of them forty days. . . " (Acts 1:3).

Just before His departure He promised that, if He went away, He would send another Comforter, even the Holy Spirit. Whereupon He "commanded them that they should not depart from Jerusalem, but wait for the promise of the Father . . ." (Acts 1:4). One hundred and twenty of those disciples gathered in an upper room to spend the time waiting and in prayer (Read Acts 1:13–15). They were together in that room for ten days (40+10) "And when the day of Pentecost was fully come . . ." (Acts 2:1). This was not something new. It was the sixth day of the third month which, according to the Jewish calendar, was the date for the annual observance of the feast of Pentecost. The day was not new, the feast was not new, but what happened on that day was; and yet not really new, but rather the fulfillment of a long-standing type.

What actually happened on *that* day of Pentecost, when the Holy Spirit came in all the fullness of His power, is seen by comparing the ritual of the feast of firstfruits with the feast of Pentecost. In the first was the presentation of the sheaf, which comprised hundreds of separate grains of corn. In the second feast, two loaves of bread were waved. A loaf of bread consisted of grains of corn ground into flour, mixed with oil, and baked in an oven, and so the separate identities were consolidated into a oneness.

Gathered in the upper room were a hundred and twenty individual believers, men and women who were prepared to be dead unto themselves, those who were ready to lose their identity for His sake. They were of one accord when the oil of God's Holy Spirit descended, and the tongues like as of fire rested upon them, and they were fused together into one body—the Church— and thus the New Testament Church was born.

Someone will say: "Were there not two loaves?" That is true. When the Spirit of God descended on those believers on the day of Pentecost, He decended upon the Jews only; but later on, in the house of Cornelius, there came another outpouring of His Spirit, this time upon the Gentiles. "While Peter yet spake these words, the Holy Ghost fell on all them which heard the Word. And they of the circumcision which believed were astonished, as many as came with Peter, because that on the Gentiles also was poured out the gift of the Holy Ghost" (Acts 10:44,45).

Later, when Peter was bearing testimony to the Church Council at Jerusalem, he said: "And as I began to speak, the Holy Ghost fell on them, as on us at the beginning" (Acts 11:15). The Lord, foreseeing that there would be two distinct outpourings of His Spirit, ordained that there should be two loaves of bread at that feast, but now in Christ Jesus there is neither Jew nor Gentile—we are one in Him.

Leaven was in those loaves because this church on earth has never been free from sin. One day it is going to be the Church in heaven. Then He will present it faultless before the Father with exceeding joy.

Spiritual Application—*Enduement of the Holy Spirit.* "For the promise is unto you, and to your children, and to all that are afar off, even as many as the Lord our God shall call" (Acts 2:39).

Here is an important subject, concerning which there are many confused minds and so it demands that it must be given honest and careful consideration. Many people will relegate this subject to the past and say that it does not concern the church of the present day. To do this one of the steps that the Lord set out for the Christian walk is being removed. This step is being turned into a barrier, and so progress, which would bring one to the end of the journey, is prevented.

Notice carefully that those early Christians were baptized with the Holy Ghost for life and for service. If Pentecost were taught as a type in the Old Testament, if Pentecost were demonstrated and the Old Testament truth ratified in the New Testament, then surely Pentecost should be taught today; and not only so, but it should be sought diligently by those who are seeking progress and accomplishment in their Christian life and service. To those who would relegate it to the past, to some other age, or to some other people, the promise was made to the Church at the time of its formation, and we are the people in this Church age. "For the promise [baptism of the Holy Spirit] is unto you [that day of Pentecost], and to your children [the next generation], and to all that are afar off [future generations and Gentiles], even as many as the Lord our God shall call" (if you have been called unto salvation, then the promise belongs to you).

Some may quote Paul that "tongues should cease." To do that is to take a text out of context, for the whole statement reads: "Charity never faileth: but whether there be prophecies, they shall fail; whether there be tongues, they shall cease; whether there be knowledge, it shall vanish away" (1 Cor. 13:8). Can it be said that prophecy has failed? Dare anyone suggest that knowledge has vanished away? Then on what grounds are tongues removed? In this statement one is by no means supporting a Tongues Movement. Where the genuine exists, the spurious can often be found. There can be no false nor counterfeit, unless there is a genuine somewhere. What we are seeking to do is to be honest with the Word of God.

One other argument should be closely examined, and that is the often repeated statement that the Lord gave "tongues" on the day of Pentecost in order to enable the disciples to preach to the foreign nationals who were gathered in Jerusalem. This is false. Firstly, the speaking in tongues was exercised by the hundred and twenty disciples in the upper room, and there were no foreign nationals in that room. Secondly, the hundred and twenty did not *preach*. The testimony of all who heard was that the disciples were magnifying the Lord: they were engaged in *worship*. Thirdly, the only person who preached that day, according to record, was Peter. He was supported by the eleven. Fourthly, the only people Peter addressed were the Jews: "Ye men of Judaea, and all ye that dwell in Jerusalem." He did not address the visitors. Therefore, the only tongue he used in preaching must have been the Jewish tongue.

Having said this as a matter of explanation, it can be left because it is not the subject under consideration. It was only an *outward* evidence. Our primary concern should be with what took place *inwardly*.

These people were changed. The timid became fearless, the weak became strong, the coward became brave, lives were changed, they went everywhere preaching the Word, and that Word was effective. The Peter who yesterday could not take the taunt of a servant girl stands and preaches with such power that three thousand souls are saved. What brought about this power? What was the source of this enabling? What was the secret that caused a handful of weak people to turn the world upside down? It was Pentecost. Before this they were believers without power—now they are believers with power.

Beloved, we are believers. We are saints, but where is our power? Let us confess that we have lost out somewhere. The church needs Pentecost, every preacher needs Pentecost, every child of God needs Pentecost, and the world is dying because there is no Pentecost. The floodgates of God's Holy Spirit have been closed, and we must ask ourselves diligently—on which side of the gates are the bolts? If we know salvation and separation, if we know sanctification, then may we allow the Lord to lead us on to Pentecost. The result will be seen in the next feast.

7

THE FEAST OF TRUMPETS

And the Lord spake unto Moses, saying, Speak unto the children of Israel, saying, In the seventh month, in the first day of the month, shall ye have a sabbath, a memorial of blowing of trumpets, an holy convocation. Ye shall do no servile work therein: but ye shall offer an offering made by fire unto the Lord (Lev. 23:23–25).

And the Lord spake unto Moses, saying, Make thee two trumpets of silver; of a whole piece shalt thou make them: that thou mayest use them for the calling of the assembly and for the journeying of the camps. And when they shall blow with them, all the assembly shall assemble themselves to thee at the door of the tabernacle of the congregation. And if they blow but with one trumpet, then the princes, which are heads of the thousands of Israel, shall gather themselves unto thee. When ye blow an alarm, then the camps that lie on the east parts shall go forward. When ye blow an alarm the second time, then the camps that lie on the south side shall take their journey: they shall blow an alarm for their journeys. But when the congregation is to be gathered together, ye shall blow, but ye shall not sound an alarm. And the sons of Aaron, the priest, shall blow with the trumpets; and they shall be to you for an ordinance for ever throughout your generations. And if ye go to war in your land against the enemy that oppresseth you, then ye shall blow an alarm with the trumpets; and ye shall be remembered before the Lord your God,

and ye shall be saved from your enemies. Also in the day
of your gladness, and in your solemn days, and in the
beginnings of your months, ye shall blow with the trumpets over your burnt offerings, and over the sacrifices of
your peace offerings; that they may be to you for a
memorial before your God: I am the Lord your God
(Num. 10:1–10).

And in the seventh month, on the first day of the
month, ye shall have an holy convocation; ye shall do no
servile work: it is a day of blowing the trumpets unto
you. And ye shall offer a burnt offering for a sweet
savour unto the Lord: one young bullock, one ram, and
seven lambs of the first year without blemish: and their
meat offering shall be of flour mingled with oil, three
tenth deals for a bullock, and two tenth deals for a ram,
and one tenth deal for one lamb, throughout the seven
lambs: and one kid of the goats for a sin offering, to
make an atonement for you: beside the burnt offering of
the month, and his meat offering, and the daily burnt
offering, and his meat offering, and their drink offerings, according unto their manner, for a sweet savour, a
sacrifice made by fire unto the Lord (Num. 29:1–6).

NO feast was observed in the fourth, fifth, or sixth months.
These would probably be the hot months of the year.

The seventh month was known as the Sabbatic month.
In it the last three feasts had to be oberved. These three,
trumpets, atonement, and tabernacles, were all included in
what was known as "tabernacles." The last journey to
Jerusalem, therefore, involved a stay of three weeks.
While the feast of tabernacles was on the first day of the
seventh month of their ecclesiastical or religious year, it
was the beginning of their civil year.

The Feast.   This cannot be described as the others because nothing special happened other than the blowing of
trumpets, and that took place at each full moon and,

therefore, was a monthly event.

A little consideration of the general practice of the blowing of trumpets might be useful. Two trumpets were always in use. These are described in the book of Numbers: "Make thee two trumpets of silver; of a whole piece shalt thou make them: that thou mayest use them for the calling of the assembly, and for the journeyings of the camps" (Num. 10:2). In later years, and at the present time, rams' horns were used, called *shophars*.

The purpose of these two trumpets was to proclaim or to announce. According to whether one trumpet sounded or two, and according to whether there were long blasts or short notes, so the people knew how to interpret and how to respond. They would know whether the trumpets were calling them to worship, to walk, or to war. They also knew whether all the tribes were involved, or only some of them. They were able to respond to those trumpets as a soldier will react to the bugle call.

In a similar way God has given to his church the two trumpets of Old and New Testaments which make up His Word. Through these Testaments He makes known His will and His purposes to all mankind. As the trumpets were made of silver so the great theme of the Bible is redemption. It is the sweet, clear sound of the gospel. As the trumpets were of one piece so there is a oneness, an entirety, a harmony, in the whole of God's Word.

The Old Testament comprises thirty-nine books, written over a period of nearly two thousand years. The many writers included kings and prophets, scribes and shepherds, teachers and servants, judges and priests, poets and singers, and many others from every walk of life—yet the Book is one.

Likewise the New Testament with its twenty-seven books, written over a period of one hundred years, declares truth recording the fulfillment of prophecies as to the future. The writers included a taxgatherer, a doctor, a fisherman, a tentmaker, and others, and yet it is one Book. Like the trumpets, the sounds and the calls are many, and yet every hearer can understand. To one comes the call to salvation, to another sanctification, to yet another guidance, reproof, encouragement, or whatever are the needs or longings of the individual.

The trumpets were used only by the priests. "And the sons of Aaron, the priests, shall blow . . ." (Num. 10:8). Only men with a divine call and the power of the Holy One resting upon them have the right to proclaim the Word of God, men who, according to Numbers 8:6–15, are called, cleansed, consecrated, and commissioned. ". ˙ ˙ No man taketh this honour unto himself, but he that is called of God, as was Aaron" (Heb. 5:4).

This, of course, does not mean the exclusion of men who cannot enter full-time ministry. God can and does qualify men in all walks of life to serve Him, but it does mean that every individual who seeks to teach the Word of God should not be a novice (1 Tim. 3:6), but one who is aware of a call and equipment.

Having considered the trumpets and the trumpeters, something should be said concerning the trumpeting.

The trumpets were sounded always on the sabbath days, at every new moon, at each festival, and on all special occasions. Some of the purposes for which trumpets were used were

Invitation—for the gathering of the people.

"And when they shall blow with them, all the assembly shall assemble themselves to thee at the door of the tabernacle of the congregation" (Num. 10:3).

Advance—when the camp should move on.

"When ye blow an alarm, then the camps that lie on the east parts shall go forward. When ye blow an alarm the second time, then the camps that lie on the south side shall take their journey . . ." (Num. 10:5,6).

Conflict—an alarm for war.

"And if ye go to war in your land against the enemy that oppresseth you, then ye shall blow an alarm with the trumpets . . ." (Num. 10:9).

Worship—announcing spiritual demands.

"Also in the day of your gladness, and in your solemn days [set feasts], and in the beginnings of your months, ye shall blow with the trumpets over your burnt offerings, and over the sacrifices of your peace offerings . . ." (Num. 10:10).

Emancipation—a joyful sound at jubilee.

"Then shalt thou cause the trumpet of the jubilee to sound on the tenth day of the seventh month, in the day of atonement shall ye make the trumpet sound throughout all your land" (Lev. 25:9).

There are some outstanding incidents with which one is well acquainted, but a reminder would help us to appreciate the idea of the trumpets. These references are to trumpets other than the two which belonged to Israel. The first sounding of a trumpet was at Sinai.

(Exod. 19:13) "When the trumpet soundeth long, they shall come up to the mount." The giving of the law was with the sounding of a trumpet.

(Rev. 4:1) ". . . and the first voice which I heard was as it were of a trumpet talking with me; which said, Come up hither, and I will shew thee things which must be hereafter." Revelation was accompanied with the sound of a trumpet.

(1 Thess. 4:16) "For the Lord Himself shall descend from heaven with a shout, with the voice of the archangel, and with the trump of God . . . ." This trumpet will be the last because we read in

(1 Cor. 15:52) "In a moment, in the twinkling of an eye, at the *last* trump: for the trumpet shall sound, and the dead

shall be raised incorruptible, and we shall be changed." This will be the final gathering—the home call.

Trumpets have discernible calls. They are readily understood by those who will listen. They are clarion calls which demand immediate obedience. Paul, when dealing with the Corinthian church concerning the vexing subject of speaking in tongues, said: "And even things without life giving sound, whether pipe or harp, except they give a distinction in the sounds, how shall it be known what is piped or harped? For if the trumpet give an uncertain sound, who shall prepare himself to the battle?" (1 Cor. 15:7,8). This is a call to a clear and distinct ministry, and it is a reminder that the Word of God—the two trumpets—has a clear and distinct message. The trouble is that too many people are too preoccupied, or have an already biased mind, to listen.

Antitype. Whereas the previous feasts have revealed historical facts, these remaining three are prophetic. This is accounted for by the fact that there has been a stepping into the seventh or sabbatic month, and also that there has been a gap of three months since the feast of Pentecost.

These feasts were all Jewish and were, and still are, celebrated by the Jewish people. Therefore the interpretation of each feast is primarily Jewish. However, there is a second lesson or application, inasmuch as they pertain to the church.

The four feasts already considered—viz: Passover, unleavened bread, firstfruits, and Pentecost, or Calvary, Emmaus walk, resurrection, and the outpouring of the Holy Spirit—are all in the past as history, while the remaining three feasts, trumpets, day of atonement, and tabernacles, or testimony, second advent, and millennium, are all in the future and are prophetic. This means that the three-month gap, which stands between the historical and the prophetical, must be the present, and that, of course, is the church.

These relationships are all summed up in two verses: "He came unto his own [the Jews], and his own received him not [Calvary]. But as many as received him [whosoever will], to them gave he power to become the sons of God [the Church], even to them that believe on his name" (John 1:11,12).

Because of this rejection of Christ by His people and the Lord's invitation to the "whosoever will," the Jewish people were dispersed and the church came into being. The Jews had rejected their Messiah; therefore, temporarily He laid them aside. Pentecost ushered in the church period, so for the Jewish nation there were the three months without any religious feast. They were rejected.

We believe that the church age is very near to its close. The coming of the Lord is at hand. The sabbatic month is about to begin; maybe it has already begun.

On the first day of this seventh month there was the sounding of the trumpets, in fact a special sounding of the trumpets so that it became an annual feast day.

Previously the ten tribes had been carried away. At the present time the whole nation, Israel and Judah, is scattered abroad. These people have not been in their land since the days when Titus destroyed the City of Jerusalem and the Temple, and carried them away into captivity. However, today the evidence around is that this nation has heard the sound of the trumpet, the clarion call that is taking them back into their own land, for we have witnessed the establishment of the State of Israeli—a nation once more.

The prophetic picture which describes this event is in the thirty-seventh chapter of Ezekiel. The prophet was caused to see a valley of dry bones, the bones very many and very dry. These represented God's people, who would be buried in the graveyard of the nations for a very long time.

The prophet was twice asked whether he thought these bones could live, and twice he referred the question back to the Lord. On each occasion the prophet was to prophesy, which he did with the accompanying results. The repeated injunction "Prophesy, son of man . . . so I prophesied" are fitted into this feast, because it could have been "Blow, son of man . . . so I blew." The two blowings would belong to the two silver trumpets.

On the first blowing bone came to his bone, flesh and sinew came upon them and skin covered them. The valley then became full of corpses.

It is suggested that this first trumpet of command has already been heard by God's people scattered across the valley of the world, because bone has been coming to bone as these people have been congregating back in their own land. Flesh, sinew, and skin have come upon them as they have developed into a nation—Israel—and taking a position among the nations, but while they have returned, they are still dead spiritually, for the Lord declared that they would return in unbelief.

At the second blowing, or prophesying, the corpses received breath and stood up a living army. If the first trumpet has already sounded, the second will not be long after, and its sounding in the prophetic program will be after the Lord has come in the air to take away His Church. This will be followed by tribulation, at the end of which the Lord will come back to this earth, His feet will stand upon the Mount of Olives, and they will behold Him whom they pierced. It will be both a day of mourning and a day of rejoicing, for they shall say: ". . . Blessed is he that cometh in the name of the Lord," as was foretold by the Lord in Matthew 23:39. At this time the nation will be reborn to become the leading nation of the world. "And I will make them one nation in the land upon the mountains of Israel; and one king shall be king to them all: and they shall be no more two nations, neither shall they be divided into two kingdoms any more at all" (Ezek. 37:22).

Spiritual Application—*Testimony.* Trumpets are heralds. They make declarations, but not of themselves. It requires living men with breath in their lungs to take up the trumpets and blow.

Having become living people through the work of the cross, having separated ourselves unto the work of the Lord, and having been filled with the fullness of His Spirit and thereby empowered, we now take up these testaments, and in the power of His Spirit, declare the Word of the Living God with a clear ringing *testimony.*

The world is surely needing someone to give it direction, for it is bewildered and hopelessly lost. Who is this someone? You, and I. "How then shall they call on him in whom they have not believed? and how shall they believe in him of whom they have not heard? and how shall they hear without a preacher? and how shall they preach, except they be sent? . . ." (Rom. 10:14,15).

The Lord give us all a Holy Ghost ministry.

8

THE DAY OF ATONEMENT

And the Lord spake unto Moses after the death of the two sons of Aaron, when they offered before the Lord, and died; and the Lord said unto Moses, Speak unto Aaron thy brother, that he come not at all times into the holy place within the vail before the mercy seat, which is upon the ark; that he die not: for I will appear in the cloud upon the mercy seat. Thus shall Aaron come into the holy place: with a young bullock for a sin offering, and a ram for a burnt offering. He shall put on the holy linen coat, and he shall have the linen breeches upon his flesh, and shall be girded with a linen girdle, and with the linen mitre shall he be attired: these are holy garments; therefore shall he wash his flesh in water, and so put them on. And he shall take of the congregation of the children of Israel two kids of the goats for a sin offering, and one ram for a burnt offering. And Aaron shall offer his bullock of the sin offering, which is for himself, and make an atonement for himself, and for his house. And he shall take the two goats, and present them before the Lord at the door of the tabernacle of the congregation. And Aaron shall cast lots upon the two goats; one lot for the Lord, and the other lot for the scapegoat. And Aaron shall bring the goat upon which the Lord's lot fell, and offer him for a sin offering. But the goat, on which the lot fell to be the scapegoat, shall be presented alive before the Lord, to make an atonement with him, and to let him go for a scapegoat into the

wilderness. And Aaron shall bring the bullock of the sin
offering, which is for himself, and shall make an atonement for himself, and for his house, and shall kill the
bullock of the sin offering which is for himself: and he
shall take a censer full of burning coals of fire from off
the altar before the Lord, and his hands full of sweet
incense beaten small, and bring it within the vail: and he
shall put the incense upon the fire before the Lord, that
the cloud of the incense may cover the mercy seat that is
upon the testimony, that he die not: and he shall take of
the blood of the bullock, and sprinkle it with his finger
upon the mercy seat eastward; and before the mercy
seat shall he sprinkle of the blood with his finger seven
times (Lev. 16:1–14).

And Aaron shall come into the tabernacle of the
congregation, and shall put off the linen garments,
which he put on when he went into the holy place, and
shall leave them there: and he shall wash his flesh with
water in the holy place, and put on his garments, and
come forth, and offer his burnt offering, and the burnt
offering of the people, and make an atonement for
himself, and for the people. And the fat of the sin
offering shall he burn upon the altar. And he that let go
the goat for the scapegoat shall wash his clothes, and
bathe his flesh in water, and afterward come into the
camp. And the bullock for the sin offering, and the goat
for the sin offering, whose blood was brought in to make
atonement in the holy place, shall one carry forth without the camp; and they shall burn in the fire their skins,
and their flesh, and their dung. And he that burneth
them shall wash his clothes, and bathe his flesh in water,
and afterward he shall come into the camp (Lev.
16:23–28).

And the Lord spake unto Moses, saying, Also on the
tenth day of this seventh month there shall be a day of
atonement: it shall be an holy convocation unto you; and
ye shall afflict your souls, and offer an offering made by

fire unto the Lord. And ye shall do no work in that same day: for it is a day of atonement, to make an atonement for you before the Lord your God. For whatsoever soul it be that shall not be afflicted in that same day, he shall be cut off from among his people. And whatsoever soul it be that doeth any work in that same day, the same soul will I destroy from among his people. Ye shall do no manner of work: it shall be a statute for ever throughout your generations in all your dwellings. It shall be unto you a sabbath of rest, and ye shall afflict your souls: in the ninth day of the month at even, from even unto even, shall ye celebrate your sabbath (Lev. 23:26–32).

THIS was the most important of all the feasts, and the most solemn day of the year; a day when, by special sacrifice, a whole year's sins were covered. This, of course, did not take the place of the Passover or make the Passover of less value. In point of fact, it was an aspect of it. It could be said that the Passover was the manward aspect, and the atonement the Godward aspect of the Cross.

The day was unique inasmuch as apart from this day there could be no continual fellowship with the Lord because of an accumulation of unconfessed and unforgiven sin throughout the year; also because the blood of bulls and goats was inadequate.

This day of humiliation, with its ceremonies, also revealed how holy God was and how distant man was. There was no immediate access to God. God was on one side of the veil and man was on the other side—the outside. The access was limited to one man, once in a year, and that under special precautionary measures. Apart from these restrictions there was immediate death, as with Nadab and Abihu.

That veil, which separated God and man, was a fabric of fine twined linen worked in blue, purple, and scarlet, fragile in itself yet formidable in its purpose (we do not accept the unscriptural and illogical four-and-a-half-inches-thick theory). It has been described by C. H. Macintosh: "Neither the Levitical priesthood nor the Levitical sacrifices could yield perfection. Insufficiency was stamped on the latter, infirmity on the former, imperfection on both. An imperfect man could not be a perfect priest, nor could an imperfect sacrifice give a perfect conscience. Aaron was not competent nor entitled to take his seat within the veil, nor could the sacrifices which he offered rend that veil."

This was the day of at-one-ment. The claims of God that man could not meet, and the needs of man that could not be satisfied, were both settled on this day, creating a oneness.

However, this still remained a temporary provision. It was only for the time being and had to be performed every year until Christ came Himself to die. It was an atonement, it was a temporary covering for sin, it was incapable of removing sin. For this reason it must always be borne in mind that the insufficiency of the atonement brought the Lord into the world. Reference is so often made to Christ's atonement. There is a hymn which says: "Christ hath for sin atonement made, what a wonderful Saviour!" This statement is incorrect. If atonement had been sufficient, Christ need not have died. Atonement only covered sin. Redemption removes sin and leaves man justified.

The Feast. There were a number of things God required of both the high priest and the people that day. It was a

Day of Humiliation. On this one day in the year, the tenth day of the seventh month, the high priest had to lay aside all his garments of glory, the breastplate and ephod, the curious girdle, and the robe with its golden bells and pomegranates, also the holy crown. "Thus shall Aaron come into the holy place . . . He shall put on the holy linen coat, and he shall have the linen breeches upon his flesh, and shall be girded with a linen girdle, and with the linen mitre shall he be attired: these are holy garments; therefore shall he wash his flesh in water, and so put them on" (Lev. 16:3,4). In this way the high priest was dressed similarly to all the priests. He had nothing of which he could boast. Outwardly he looked the same as all the priests, although inwardly he still remained the high priest.

Once in the end of the age, the great High Priest, our Lord Jesus Christ, laid aside all the glory that He had with the Father from before the foundation of the earth, put upon Himself the plain robe of humanity, and becoming like one of us, He humbled Himself. That is, outwardly and actually Jesus became man, but essentially He remained the divine Son of God because His divinity is something He cannot and will not forfeit. It was a

Day of Imputation. Two goats were taken to become one offering; one was for God and the other for man. There were also a young bullock and a ram. These were an offering for the priest for he, too, like the people, was imperfect and needed his offering. This is where the high priest differed from the great High Priest, where man is different from Him who became man. Jesus needed no offering for Himself and, therefore, Himself became our Offering.

A casting of lots took place for the two goats. The animal that fell out to the Lord became the sacrificial one and had to die. The other became the scapegoat. The sins of the people were confessed, as Aaron laid his hands heavily on the head of the goat. This was an act of identification and imputation. The sins of the people had passed to the animal. It was then taken into the wilderness and lost, and as the goat became lost so, likewise, were the sins that it had carried. Jesus paid the price of our sin, which is death—"The wages of sin is death"—and He also removed our sins as far as the east is from the west, to be remembered against us no more. It was a

Day of Substitution. "And Aaron shall lay both his hands upon the head of the live goat, and confess over him all the iniquities of the children of Israel, and all their transgressions in all their sins, putting them upon the head of the goat, and shall send him away by the hand of a fit man into the wilderness: And the goat shall bear upon him all their iniquities unto a land not inhabited: and he shall let go the goat in the wilderness" (Lev. 16:21,22).

This was substitution, or one taking the place of another. "... And the Lord hath laid on Him the iniquity of us all" (Isa. 53:6). "For He hath made Him to be sin for us, who knew no sin; that we might be made the righteousness of God in Him" (2 Cor. 5:21). It was a

Day of Lonely Service. "And there shall be no man in the tabernacle of the congregation when he goeth in to make atonement in the holy place, until he come out, and have made an atonement for himself, and for his household, and for all the congregation of Israel" (Lev. 16:17).

No man was allowed to enter into the tabernacle on that day, save the high priest alone. He went in, a solitary figure taking in the blood of the bullock, firstly for himself, and then entering again with the blood of the goat which was for the people. How significant that none of the priests, nor yet the sons of Levi, could be within the tabernacle! Jesus trod the winepress alone, forsaken of God and rejected of men. God had nothing to do with the making of man's first covering (aprons of fig leaves); man had nothing to do with the making of the second covering.

> Jesus, Thy blood and righteousness,
> My beauty are, my glorious dress.

This day was a
Day of Acceptance. On this day alone, with shed blood,

the High Priest was allowed to pass beyond the veil, while the whole congregation waited anxiously outside. Before passing beyond the veil, the high priest would drop incense upon the censer, and then hold the censer at arm's length within the veil. When the fragrant smoke from the incense had filled the place and dimmed the sight of the mercy seat and the glory cloud, then the high priest entered with the blood. This blood he sprinkled seven times upon the mercy seat, signifying a perfect acceptance with God through applied blood. Then, taking a step backwards, he sprinkled the blood seven times before the ark, meaning a perfect standing before God through shed blood.

Jesus, having accomplished His work of redemption upon the cross ". . . by *his own blood* he entered in once into the holy place, having obtained eternal redemption for us" (Heb. 9:12). "For Christ is not entered into the holy places made with hands, which are the figures of the true; but into heaven itself, now to appear in the presence of God for us" (Heb. 9:24). It was a

Day of Soul Affliction. "And this shall be a statute for ever unto you: that in the seventh month, on the tenth day of the month, ye shall afflict your souls, and do no work at all, whether it be one of your own country, or a stranger that sojourneth among you" (Lev. 16:29).

This meant a day of sorrow, repentance, confession of sin, a period of a broken and a contrite spirit. It was a

Day of Rest. "Ye shall do no work in that same day" (Lev. 16:28). "It shall be unto you a sabbath of rest" (Lev. 23:32).

We need to stand still and see the salvation of the Lord. We do nothing because we are nothing. It is when we rest from strugglings, strivings, and all the works of the flesh, that we can appreciate and appropriate His Work on our behalf.

O give Thine own sweet rest to me,
That I may speak with soothing power,
A word in season, as from Thee,
To weary ones in needful hour.

Finally, it was a

Day of Accomplishment. Such a day must have results. "For on that day shall the priest make an atonement for you, to cleanse you, that ye may be clean from all your sins before the Lord" (Lev. 16:30).

Coming out from the tabernacle to the great concourse of people that waited outside, the high priest lifted his hands in blessing over the assembly, and cried: "Ye are clean from all your sins," and so the day concluded.

Jesus has accomplished the same work and has made the same pronouncement to all who are washed in his precious blood. "Now ye are clean through the word which I have spoken unto you" (John 15:3).

Antitype. Israel had been at variance with God through many years and many apostasies. There has been no relationship since they rejected Christ as their Messiah, their King. The nation has been scattered, a veil has been over their faces and darkness in their minds. Paul says: "But their minds were blinded: for until this day remaineth the same vail untaken away in the reading of the Old Testament; which vail is done away in Christ. But even unto this day, when Moses is read, the vail is upon their heart. Nevertheless when it shall turn to the Lord, the vail shall be taken away" (2 Cor. 3:14–16).

The evidence is that, at the moment, there is need of an at-one-ment. This takes place after the trumpets, when the nation returns to its land and the Lord comes to the Mount of Olives, and they recognize Him as their Messiah and He will acknowledge them as His people.

Spiritual Application—*The rapture.* For the believer,

this will be the second advent of our Lord Jesus Christ. At the moment things are not what they should be; the world is upside down, the church is lukewarm, and the Christian indifferent. We are undoubtedly in the Laodicean period of church history, concerning which it has been declared that we are neither hot nor cold. The present conditions were outlined by Paul to Timothy: "This know also, that in the last days perilous times shall come. For men shall be lovers of their own selves, covetous, boasters, proud, blasphemers, disobedient to parents, unthankful, unholy, without natural affection, truce-breakers, false accusers, incontinent, fierce, despisers of those that are good, traitors, heady, highminded, lovers of pleasures more than lovers of God; having a form of godliness, but denying the power thereof: from such turn away. . . . But evil men and seducers shall wax worse and worse, deceiving, and being deceived" (2 Tim. 3:1–5,13).

There is not a statement here which is not in full bloom right now. Satan is having his harvest. Evil is dominating our world of society, and righteousness is suppressed on every hand. The saint is persecuted for righteousness' sake. Much of the church is being governed by the world, by the World Council of Churches, when the church should be governing the world by example and precept.

There is great need of an adjustment, an at-one-ment. This will take place when the Lord returns to this earth. At that time wrongs will be righted, sin will be dealt with, saints will reign, and the Lord will be honored.

We have been saved spirit, soul, and body, but at the moment the body is out of harmony. It is still carnal, it bears the marks of suffering, it knows the limitations of the mortal, but when Christ comes, the mortal shall put on immortality, the corruptible shall put on incorruption, and this earthly body will be changed into a spiritual body, so that the body will be in harmony with the soul and the spirit. All the things of the earth, the weaknesses and the failings, will be covered—yea, removed. We shall be clean from everything. Our great day of atonement will have come in order to fit us for the feast of tabernacles.

9

THE FEAST OF TABERNACLES

And the Lord spake unto Moses, saying, Speak unto
the children of Israel, saying, The fifteenth day of this
seventh month shall be the feast of tabernacles for seven
days unto the Lord. On the first day shall be an holy
convocation: ye shall do no servile work therein. Seven
days ye shall offer an offering made by fire unto the
Lord: on the eighth day shall be an holy convocation
unto you; and ye shall offer an offering made by fire
unto the Lord: it is a solemn assembly; and ye shall do no
servile work therein. These are the feasts of the Lord,
which ye shall proclaim to be holy convocations, to offer
an offering made by fire unto the Lord, a burnt offering,
and a meat offering, a sacrifice, and drink offerings,
every thing upon his day: beside the sabbaths of the
Lord, and beside your gifts, and beside all your vows,
and beside all your freewill offerings, which ye give unto
the Lord. Also in the fifteenth day of the seventh month,
when ye have gathered in the fruit of the land, ye shall
keep a feast unto the Lord seven days: on the first day
shall be a sabbath, and on the eighth day shall be a
sabbath. And ye shall take you on the first day the
boughs of goodly trees, branches of palm trees, and the
boughs of thick trees, and willows of the brook; and ye
shall rejoice before the Lord your God seven days. And
ye shall keep it a feast unto the Lord seven days in the
year. It shall be a statute for ever in your generations: ye
shall celebrate it in the seventh month. Ye shall dwell in

booths seven days; all that are Israelites born shall dwell in booths: that your generations may know that I made the children of Israel to dwell in booths, when I brought them out of the land of Egypt: I am the Lord your God. And Moses declared unto the children of Israel the feasts of the Lord (Lev. 23:33–44).

And on the second day were gathered together the chief of the fathers of all the people, the priests, and the Levites, unto Ezra the scribe, even to understand the words of the law. And they found written in the law which the Lord had commanded by Moses, that the children of Israel should dwell in booths in the feast of the seventh month: and that they should publish and proclaim in all their cities, and in Jerusalem, saying, Go forth unto the mount, and fetch olive branches, and pine branches, and myrtle branches, and palm branches, and branches of thick trees, to make booths, as it is written. So the people went forth, and brought them, and made themselves booths, every one upon the roof of his house, and in their courts, and in the courts of the house of God, and in the street of the water gate, and in the street of the gate of Ephraim. And all the congregation of them that were come again out of the captivity made booths, and sat under the booths: for since the days of Jeshua the son of Nun unto that day had not the children of Israel done so. And there was very great gladness. Also day by day, from the first day unto the last day, he read in the book of the law of God. And they kept the feast seven days; and on the eighth day was a solemn assembly, according unto the manner (Neh. 8:13–18).

THE very title of this last feast suggests to the mind something of rest and fellowship. While it did remind them of the pilgrimage of the past and God's faithfulness, the joy of the feast was the anticipation of that day when journeyings will have terminated and rest will be permanent.

It was to them as the Lord's Table is to the believer. In

that feast we look back to Calvary, and remember what it meant to Him to bring us out of the bondage of the past and to direct us along this pilgrim way, but it is also "till He come." We anticipate the time when we will sit with Him and feast on heaven's glories, with none to make us afraid.

It was not only the last feast, which terminated their ecclesiastical year, but it was also the longest feast, lasting eight days, from a sabbath to a sabbath. It was the most joyous of all the feasts coming after the one of greatest solemnity, and thereby made a wonderful consummation. The joyous things of life are always more appreciable when they have been preceded by a dark or difficult experience. "Weeping may endure for a night, but joy cometh in the morning."

In Deuteronomy 16:13,14 it is stated: "Thou shalt observe the feast of tabernacles seven days, after that thou hast gathered in thy corn and thy wine: and thou shalt rejoice in thy feast, thou, and thy son, and thy daughter, and thy manservant, and thy maidservant, and the Levite, the stranger, and the fatherless, and the widow, that are within thy gates."

This was an all-inclusive feast, no one was left out. It was sometimes called the feast of ingathering because it was the end of summer, and work in the fields was finished, and the time had come when they could relax and rejoice.

The evidence is that the nation went a long time without keeping this feast, somewhere in the region of 800 to 900 years. This is stated in Neh. 8:17: "And all the congregation of them that were come again out of the captivity made booths, and sat under the booths: for since the days of Jeshua the son of Nun unto that day had not the children of Israel done so."

Seeing they could not keep the feast until after they had left their tent life in the wilderness and established themselves in the land, there could be a question as to whether

they had made any practice of this command until their
return from captivity.

The Feast. "And ye shall take you on the first day the
boughs of goodly trees, branches of palm trees, and the
boughs of thick trees, and willows of the brook; and ye
shall rejoice before the Lord your God seven days. . . . Ye
shall dwell in booths seven days; all that are Israelites
born shall dwell in booths" (Lev. 23:40,42).

For seven days all the residents of Israel left their homes
in order to dwell in temporary booths. The purpose of this
was that the people should have a constant reminder of the
forty years when the nation dwelt in tents wandering in the
wilderness with no home; how the Lord had made full
provision in all things, so that not one good thing had
failed; also that the Lord Himself had become a pilgrim
with them and had tabernacled in their midst, leading
them by the pillar of cloud and fire, and had brought them
into the land He had promised.

Then there was the anticipation. These were a people
who would always wander the face of the earth. True, it
would be as a result of their own rebellion and idolatry, but
in all the wanderings they were to keep this feast to remind
them that there would be a day when those wanderings
would end, and they would possess their own land, build
their own houses, plant their own vineyards, and sit under
their own fig trees, because the promise was: "There remaineth therefore a rest to the people of God" (Heb. 4:9).

We have read of the trees to be used in the building of
these booths. Nehemiah adds to the number: ". . . Go
forth unto the mount, and fetch olive branches, and pine
branches, and myrtle branches, and palm branches, and
branches of thick trees, to make booths, as it is written" (8:
15).

Many of the trees used are symbolic. The thick trees
would speak of shade and of divine protection. The palm

has always been the emblem of victory, as the olive has been used for peace. It also represented fatness and plenty. The willow of the brook signified a thriving and a blessed people planted by the rivers of water. All these things, while reminiscent, foreshadow the wonderful millennial age, when men shall dwell in peace and safety, and none shall make them afraid.

Numbers 29 lists the number of animals to be used in the sacrifices of that week. The bullocks, diminishing in number from day to day for the eight days, were 13, 12, 11, 10, 9, 8, 7, 1. It has been suggested that the decrease to one would foretell, in fact declare, how the many sacrifices of the law would, in the fullness of time, be reduced to the One Sacrifice that was to be made once in the end of the age. The anticipated peace would only come through the peace of the Cross.

There is a constant repetition in all of the references to the joy and rejoicing of the occasion, the gifts sent to each other. On the last day of the feast were special celebrations and joy. While the sacrifice, the diminished sacrifice, of this day was being prepared, the priest, accompanied by a procession of singing people, went down to the pool of Siloam. There he drew water with a golden pitcher which they brought back to the temple, where the water was poured out into one of two silver bowls at the altar. The other bowl contained the wine of the drink offering. These would be poured out before the Lord as the feast ended.

In this connection, during the Lord's public ministry, He went up to Jerusalem on every occasion when it was required of all the males. One of these occasions is recorded in John and concerns this feast. "Now the Jews' feast of tabernacles was at hand. His brethren therefore said unto him, Depart hence, and go into Judæa, that thy disciples also may see the works that thou doest. For there is no man that doeth anything in secret, and he himself

seeketh to be known openly. If thou do these things, shew
thyself to the world. For neither did his brethren believe in
him. Then Jesus said unto them, My time is not yet come.
... Go ye up unto this feast: I go not up yet unto this feast;
for my time is not yet full come.... But when his brethren
were gone up, then went he also up unto the feast, not
openly, but as it were in secret.... Now about the midst of
the feast Jesus went up into the temple, and taught.... In
the last day, that great day of the feast, Jesus stood and
cried, saying, If any man thirst, let him come unto me, and
drink. He that believeth on me, as the scripture hath said,
out of his belly shall flow rivers of living water (But this
spake he of the Spirit, which they that believe on him
should receive) ..." (John 7:2-39).

Thus the Lord was turning the thoughts of the people
away from the shadow to the substance, away from ritual
to reality.

Antitype. He who delivered will yet deliver. As surely as
God brought them through the wilderness experience, the
tent dwelling, and the wanderings, into the promised land
(which thing they were not to forget because He had given
the promised land to Abraham and to his seed for an
everlasting inheritance), so surely the Jews are to realize in
this present dispensation that they are still pilgrims and
strangers, they are still a wandering people away from
their permanent address.

The apostle writing to the Hebrews said: "Let us therefore fear, lest, a promise being left us of entering into his
rest, any of you should seem to come short of it.... Seeing
therefore it remaineth that some must enter therein, and
they to whom it was first preached entered not in because
of unbelief.... There remaineth therefore a rest to the
people of God" (4:1-9). That rest is the millennial rest,
when for a thousand years they will dwell in peace, and
concerning which it is stated "But in the last days it shall

come to pass, that the mountain of the house of the Lord shall be established in the top of the mountains, and it shall be exalted above the hills; and people shall flow unto it. And many nations shall come, and say, Come, and let us go up to the mountain of the Lord, and to the house of the God of Jacob; and he will teach us of his ways, and we will walk in his paths: for the law shall go forth of Zion, and the word of the Lord from Jerusalem. And he shall judge among many people, and rebuke strong nations afar off; and they shall beat their swords into plowshares, and their spears into pruning-hooks: nation shall not lift up a sword against nation, neither shall they learn war any more. But they shall sit every man under his vine and under his fig tree; and none shall make them afraid: for the mouth of the Lord of hosts hath spoken it. For all people will walk every one in the name of his god, and we will walk in the name of the Lord our God for ever and ever" (Mic. 4:1–5).

"The wolf also shall dwell with the lamb, and the leopard shall lie down with the kid; and the calf and the young lion and the fatling together; and a little child shall lead them. And the cow and the bear shall feed; their young ones shall lie down together: and the lion shall eat straw like the ox. And the sucking child shall play on the hole of the asp, and the weaned child shall put his hand on the cockatrice' den. They shall not hurt nor destroy in all my holy mountain: for the earth shall be full of the knowledge of the Lord, as the waters cover the sea" (Isa. 11:6–9).

Spiritual Application—*Heaven.* The life of the Christian is a journey. This journey we have followed. It is one of achievement and attainment, a going on with the Lord in deeper experiences and fuller, richer fellowship. With Paul we say: "I press toward the mark for the prize of the high calling of God in Christ Jesus" (Phil. 3:14). "Looking unto Jesus the author and finisher of our faith; who for the joy that was set before him endured the cross, despising the shame, and is set down at the right hand of the throne of God" (Heb. 12:2).

May we ask you, reader, where are you along this wondrous path? Here are the steps—salvation, leading to separation and consecration, then receiving the fullness of the Holy Spirit, whereby we bear our testimony, until the Lord come, and heaven is our home.

Having decided our position, may the Lord enable us to step forward into a fuller experience.

> O, walk with God, whilst thou on earth
> With pilgrim steps must fare,
> Content to leave the world its mirth
> And claim no dwelling there.
> O stranger, thou must seek a home
> Beyond the fearful tide;
> And if to Canaan thou wouldst come,
> O, Who but God can guide?

SUMMARY

April 14:
  Passover—Calvary—Salvation.
April 15:
  Unleavened Bread—Emmaus Walk—Separation.
April 16:
  Firstfruits—Resurrection—Consecration.
June 6:
  Pentecost—Pentecost—Holy Spirit.
October 1:
  Trumpets—Regathering of Israel—Testimony.
October 10:
  Atonement—Return of Messiah—Rapture.
October 15–22:
  Tabernacles—Millennium—Heaven.